Praise for *Lead Without Limits: How Inspirational Leaders Make the Impossible Probable*

"*Lead Without Limits* is a refreshingly practical and deeply inspiring guide to modern leadership. Grounded in research and rich with real-world examples, it redefines leadership as an everyday act of inspiration—available to anyone willing to grow others while growing themselves."

—**Marc Effron**, President, Talent Strategy Group

"*Lead Without Limits* is a thoughtful and credible guide to unlocking leadership potential, blending real-world insights with practical strategies. It challenges conventional thinking, encouraging leaders to be mindful, not mindless, in how they develop themselves and others. The use of relatable stories and powerful reflections helps readers connect the content to their own experiences—both the wins and the challenges. This book inspires leaders at all levels to elevate their teams, reduce unproductive drama, and build a sustainable path to success. A valuable resource for anyone committed to meaningful leadership growth."

—**Terry Simmons**, Former Chief Procurement Officer, AbbVie

"Inspirational Leadership is the key to greatness in organizations. While such leadership may seem rare, that need not be the case; there is so much potential that goes unrecognized or undeveloped.

The significant premise of this book is that inspirational leadership can be developed and nurtured, anywhere. It identifies the elements of inspirational leadership and provides a simple, practical, and actionable framework to understand inspirational leadership in real life, irrespective of the station of the subject. Going further, it provides organizations with the tools for enabling development and nurturing of such leadership.

The underlying proven concepts and the elegant engineering of the Enluma Leadership Model make it intuitive and actionable. By focusing on all levels of the organization, the Enluma Leadership Model is ideal for organizations that are already on a path of transformation, as well as those that are seeking the sparks for change to come from within; I would consider my organization to belong to the former category, and intend to empower my organization with this approach."

—**Herald Manjooran**, Founder and CEO at DivIHN Integration, Inc.

"Chris Sprague has broken new ground in his practical and helpful book, *Lead Without Limits*. In leadership literature, few researchers have attempted to wrap their arms around the important question, 'What is inspirational leadership?' Through original research, Chris has distilled then described the behavioral science and art of inspirational leadership. This book is packed with rich wisdom for everyone hungry to inspire, and the contents of this book can be reread over the course of one's career and still find fresh and practical insights. In *Lead Without Limits* the author has provided a developmental pathway for leaders at every level of an organization to grow in effectively inspiring their people to dream more, learn more, do more, and become more. I have personally benefitted from *Lead Without Limits*, and I highly recommend this book to you."

— **Dennis W. Stranges**, PhD, CEO, Insight Coaching & Consulting

"In my work with leaders and teams, I've seen the urgent need to redefine what inspirational leadership looks like —especially as we work to build future leadership benches and meet the evolving expectations of new generations in the workforce. *Lead Without Limits* rises to that challenge. Offering a research-based, real-world framework that reimagines leadership as a daily practice of purpose, trust, and meaningful impact. This book provides a wonderful guide to building this capacity in yourself and your organization and offers real life examples on how to implement these practices. The Enluma Leadership Model is a practical and timely guide for anyone committed to growing leaders who inspire from the inside out."

— **Aimee Daniels**, Master Chair & Best Practice Chair,
   Vistage International

"I've read any number of leadership books over the years. *Lead Without Limits* stands out for its clarity of vision and strategic development. It not only outlines a compelling vision, but also charts a practical, values-driven path forward with indispensable practical examples woven throughout. Chris turns abstract ideas into actionable insights and tangible results-oriented offerings, providing a framework that is both inspiring and imminently practical. I look forward to putting the Enluma Leadership Model into practice in our business!"

— **Eric Hersey**, Founder and CEO, The Spanish Touch

LEAD
Without
LIMITS

*How Inspirational Leaders
Make the Improbable Possible*

by

Christopher Sprague, PhD

Contributing Author: Jan Leeuwinga

ISBN 978-1-965438-06-0

Library of Congress Control Number: 2025908157

Published by Soro Publishing

For more information about our books and authors, visit our website: www. soropublishing.com.

Preface

Why are some groups more motivated and energized?

Why do some groups readily achieve incredible results?

Why do some leaders innately inspire and elevate their teams?

We became obsessed with these three questions and believe they are key to a more effective and fulfilling future—a future in which energized, motivated, and productive organizations, powered by inspirational leadership, are admired for their competitive advantage and immense potential.

Would you like to unleash a more motivating and energizing future for yourself and your organization?

Table of Contents

Introduction

6,059 kilometers or 3,765 miles

This is the distance between Fort Washington, Pennsylvania, in the United States and Roden, the Netherlands, our two hometowns.

Even though we were separated by this large distance, unknowingly we were headed down similar paths, paths that embraced the rewarding opportunity to lead teams and develop people in large global organizations for both immediate and longer-term success. We shared a passion for the challenge and reward of (1) supporting people to grow and (2) helping them to achieve what they did not think was possible. This combination resulted in people happily bringing their best, teams enjoying their work, and an environment where targets and goals are exceeded. Is this a folktale, legend, or myth? On the contrary, this is an attainable and critical goal for every organization: to operate in an environment of inspirational leaders who care for their teams and dare to transform.

Our paths eventually crossed in the US while working for the same Fortune 100 company. To kick us off on the upcoming journey, we thought it would be beneficial to head back to our hometowns to first share our personal experiences with inspirational leadership.

Christopher Sprague

In September of 1993, another school year was starting at Upper Dublin High School in Ft. Washington, Pennsylvania. My senior year class load included German, Anatomy/Physiology, Government, and English. To illustrate my degree of nerditude, the class I was most excited to take was…Calculus. And, the key reason for my excitement was the teacher, Mr. Michael Gurysh, who'd been a favorite teacher of other math classes. Mr. Gurysh's class was not 55 minutes of lecture and boredom while you counted the minutes until the bell rang. Instead, Mr. Gurysh's class was a level playing field (where everyone was called Mr. or Ms. using their last name). The hour was filled with humor, everyone was largely engaged, and he made complex concepts fun and easy to understand.

In calculus you commonly have answers of one or zero. Not in Mr. Gurysh's class. Instead of an answer being one, it was our Spanish friend Juan (one) and instead of zero, it was the number of Ms. Sandstrom's friends (a peer in our class). (Side note: Ms. Sandstorm is a lovely person and a friend who didn't mind Mr. Gurysh's humor.) If you were daydreaming out the window, he would ask you to come back from planet Mongo and join us on Earth.

I remember one day I asked if I could eat my lunch in class as I had a meeting during my lunch period. While eating an apple in the front of the class, Mr. Gurysh stopped the class, looked at me and said, "drosophila melanogaster," and then went back to teaching. We all stopped, bewildered. Realizing we were confused, Mr. Gurysh then stopped and said, "the common fruit fly," causing the room to erupt in laughter. Mr. Gurysh established a safe and enjoyable space where we could ask questions, learn, laugh, and work hard. Through this style, he made one of the hardest classes in our school fun—so much so, we looked forward to going to calculus every day.

I realized just how much of an impact Mr. Gyrush had on me six months after his class ended.

- In December of 1994, I had just finished Calculus 1 at the University of Delaware. Because of the confidence Mr. Gurysh instilled, I chose to take a harder math class than required for a biology major. He subtly challenged me to be better even after I was out of his class.

- In most college classes, the content of a yearlong high school class was typically covered in the first three to four weeks. After that first month, you were introduced to more complex topics or areas that you had not seen in high school. At the end of the first semester of college calculus, I realized that we had covered more than a semester of college calculus in Mr. Gurysh's class. While we enjoyed the class every day, we were very productive and effective.

At the end of 1994, I was even more impressed with his ability to lead us, to cover so much content, and make it enjoyable at the same time. Mr. Gurysh showed me what was possible through effective leadership. Now almost thirty years later, I have realized Mr. Gurysh was my first experience with the power of inspirational leadership.

Jan Leeuwinga

I grew up in the Northern part of the Netherlands, in a small town called Roden, approximately 10,000 strong. As a young boy, and this likely applies to most of Western European countries, there was only one sport to join, which is *voetbal* (commonly known in the US as *soccer*). While I was marginally successful at *voetbal*, at 14 I decided to try my luck with basketball, a sport, certainly back in the 1990s, that was not very popular in the Netherlands. This may strike you as odd because googling "tallest country in the world" will direct you to the Netherlands with the following descriptor: "The Netherlands is also known as the land of giants." Perhaps basketball is a missed opportunity? Regardless, I quickly discovered that my combination of ball control, speed, and accurate shooting were the key ingredients for success in the game of basketball. At age 16, I was "recruited" (more likely asked, but for my ego I'd like to think recruited) to join a more professional youth team and to take the game more seriously.

This is when I first was introduced to Henri and Dick, my two coaches. To paint their coaching picture: both gentlemen were not certified coaches with titles and historic successes; rather they maintained regular day jobs (construction and IT). Importantly, they shared an incredible passion for the game of basketball and a vision for basketball in Roden. Ten teenagers joined on the journey, one that none of us initially truly understood. Now years later, I can reflect on Henri and Dick's leadership and appreciate their impact.

Two words are forever branded in my brain: *conditioning* and *fundamentals*. Why may you ask? That full summer, day in and day out, we ran through parks, woods, and trails. While many of my non-basketball friends spent their summertime at the water, near the local lakes, mine was spent pushing my body to its limits with "one more 15 km run." So, you wonder, why go through this effort and pain? Was it human perseverance? Competitiveness? Comradery? Fueled and inspired by Henri and Dick's leadership, I would say yes to all the above. Toward the end of summer, I was excited that the gyms opened, and we were able to transition to an indoor setting. Little did I realize indoor conditioning took a totally different form—suicide drills and pistol Pete feet among the favorites. As the leaves started to turn color, the time came that we finally got a basketball in our hands. Countless dribbling drills, no-contact ball movement, and simple passing games followed, all building the foundation needed to win any game in basketball. None of us knew that, but our coaches did.

The results were astonishing:

1. We earned a promotion to the regional league in year two and the national league in year three. (Promotion once in four years is quite an accomplishment; being promoted twice in that same timeframe was very rare.)

2. Early on in year two, we beat the "Donar Kids," the professional youth basketball organization in the Northern part of the Netherlands known to feed the professional men's league and national team. To this day I remember these arrogant kids coming into our gym with condescending looks toward our equipment and overall setup. The team had incredible individual talented players, but we beat them by three points. Why did we beat them? We were better conditioned with more sound fundamentals, but the grueling work and efforts during the summer brought together a team that was willing to fight for each other and relied on each other.

3. In year three, we joined an international tournament in which all the top European teams took part. We were an add-on due to a late cancellation of a team from Slovenia. No one expected us to do well, but we made it out of the group stage in second place and ended up finishing third place in the tournament.

While I did not realize years ago, the key to our success was the inspirational leadership of my two coaches. Later in the book we will discuss the layers of inspirational leadership, so take this as a "teaser." At the organizational level they had an aspiration or a vision for what they wanted this team to accomplish. Together, they crafted a strategy and a roadmap on how we would get there. As part of this strategy, they identified their responsibilities, and they determined the milestones and requirements for success. Each one of us had an assigned role on the team, and the coaches purposefully balanced personalities and assignments. At an individual level, each player took responsibility for his assignment and his role on the team. Each player was aware of his core strengths, and the environment invited us to demonstrate individual leadership and ultimately achieve personal and team success.

Through this experience, I realized that leadership is all around us, and every individual can be a leader. My initial exposure was sports-based, which is perhaps an obvious choice, but I challenge you to reflect on examples of inspirational leadership in your experiences. Inspirational leadership, if applied with structure and consistency, can generate personal, team, and organizational success, and it is the key to potential value at an individual, team, and organizational level.

Our Combined Experience

Reflecting on these two personal experiences, there are overlapping elements. It raises important questions: Why would teams happily work hard across multiple years to achieve what would seem lofty or near impossible? Why isn't every job or experience like this? Here is the crazy part: in putting the contents of this book together, nearly everyone we surveyed in our research shared similar stories about being part of special groups that were very successful, personally fulfilling, and a lot of fun; sadly, the examples of these magical groups were not common in their professional work.

While we personally have seen the benefits of this powerful inspirational leadership connection, we identified five core questions to answer:

- **When people say "leader," what do they mean?**

- **Why don't we have a model enabling the development of inspirational leaders?**

- **What are the key elements of inspirational leadership?**

- **How can we more intentionally develop leaders who energize and inspire?**

- **Why don't we expect that every group and role is successful, fulfilling, and enjoyable?**

Herein lies the purpose of this book. We wanted to understand the leadership driving these successful teams and how we can help leaders start and progress their journey inspiring themselves and others. What we did not want to do is bore you with theory, theoretical models, and impractical examples. We want this book to be practical, so you come away with clear steps to take for yourself and to better help others.

Building on our experience leading others, we conducted a research study asking people from different industries, generations, and backgrounds about their experiences. On the basis of these combined insights, we developed the Enluma Leadership Model, which is robust yet practical. Our model differentiates the approach to inspire yourself, peers, stakeholders, direct reports, and organizations because the approach does differ. Other models take a one-size fits all approach for all leaders or focus solely on senior leaders (c-suites).

We tested the model against our experience, our research, industry experts, and literature at the intersection of exceptional leadership and exemplary teams.

We are excited that our leadership model can serve as a practical catalyst to ignite and support your journey toward becoming an inspirational leader.

Partnership with You

Our model is practical and quick to apply for leaders regardless of their role, experience, or organization's size. If you're reading this book, you're looking to improve individually, in leading a team of direct reports, and/or in leading an organization with multiple levels. We also know that being a first-time supervisor or manager is tough. In many cases you've gone from being a peer to now being "the boss." That is challenging, and we want to provide tools to help.

For leaders new to being in charge of an organization or struggling to move forward with a vision, we want to give the keys to unlock the potential. This does not require implementing expensive IT systems or complex models, but rather high-value adjustments in thinking, mindsets, and focus.

This is our partnership with you. We want to equip you with a flexible framework that enables leaders, teams, and organizations to be more energized and motivated while achieving improbable results.

Overview of the Book

In this book, we will guide you through four parts.

In **Part 1: The Current State of Leadership** we explore and challenge the current state of leadership. We delve into the potential impacts of a leader, good and bad, and align on a fundamental question: What is a leader? We have gathered and summarized key concepts from the last twenty years to give you a concise and comprehensive state of leadership today and why it is critical to take a different approach going forward.

In **Part 2: The Enluma Leadership Model**, we take you through our study results (including some surprising ones) and our insights to better understand what defines enjoyable and productive workgroups. We present the four key elements of inspirational leadership. Additionally, we introduce the leadership layers: Foundational Leadership, leading ourselves and others; People Leadership, leading direct reports; and Organizational Leadership, leading multiple levels of people. We consider these layers additive (not isolated), which means that a good organizational leader is also a good people and foundational leader. Finally, we reveal the glue that holds the model together.

In **Part 3: The Enluma Leadership Model in Practice**, we illustrate how the model works for each of the three leadership layers with each of the elements. Each element/layer combination contains a fundamental foundation, and we have developed prompting questions for each of the twelve themes that underpin inspirational leadership. The questions will challenge your mindset and assumptions and fuel your progress on your journey to be an inspirational leader.

Part 4: Your Journey guides you to illuminate your path to inspirational leadership. You can use the assessments to understand where you are and use our resources to build your personal roadmap. Here, we will challenge you to identify opportunity areas and provide important tips to manage challenges and setbacks and make your journey a success.

PART 1

The Current State of Leadership

CHAPTER 1

A Leader's Impact

*"A leader takes people where they want to go.
A great leader takes people where they don't
necessarily want to go, but ought to be."*
—Rosalynn Carter

The Art of Possible with Strong Leadership

On April 5, 1937, in Harlem, NY, recent Jamaican immigrants Luther and Maud Powell welcomed their second child, Colin Luther Powell, into the world. Growing up in multiple boroughs of New York City, he was an average athlete and a good student, and came from modest means[1]. For college, he attended the City College of New York (CCNY), majoring in Geology where he found his passion, the Reserve Officers Training Corps (ROTC) program. The ROTC program provided structure and purpose that impacted Mr. Powell for the remainder of his life. From the ROTC program at CCNY, Mr. Powell worked his way up through the ranks of the Army to become the national security advisor for President Ronald Reagan, the Chairman of the Joint Chiefs of Staff for President George H.W. Bush, and then Secretary of State for President George W. Bush. Based on his military and government service and his community service, he has received accolades and awards from numerous groups around the world. There are even elementary schools in the United States and streets in Germany named after him. Coming from his modest means, he was the definition of the American Dream. If you listen to his talks or read any of his books (highly recommended), it's clear that Mr. Powell understood the value of leadership and the role it played in his success.

In 2011, then White House fellow Amy Wilkinson, asked Mr. Powell a provocative question,[2] "How does (Mr. Powell) define the key characteristics of leadership that make you an advocate for good?" Mr. Powell's immediate response was, "trust... and creating conditions of trust in an organization. Good leaders are trusted by followers." Then he illustrated the ultimate value of a leader: "Leaders take organizations past the level that the science of management says is possible." In essence, teams and organizations led by good leaders can achieve what some consider improbable or even impossible.

What makes Colin Powell's story even more powerful is the time periods in which he achieved these accomplishments. He attended CCNY in the late 1950s and attended military training in the 1960s. While the military integrated earlier than the rest of the country, Mr. Powell encountered and endured a turbulent and racially divided country. In his book, *My American Journey*, Mr. Powell noted that in 1964 he was stationed at Fort Benning in Georgia. On the way home one night, he was hungry for a cheeseburger and went to a local fast-food restaurant. They refused to serve him and told him to go to the back window where they would hand him a cheeseburger. Looking back at it now, it seems insane that a restaurant would refuse to serve Colin Powell. Even the 1980s and 1990s still represented a time when there were not many black or Jamaican-Americans in the higher roles in the government or the military. Throughout all of this, Mr. Powell was seen as a man of dignity and respect who used the positive impact of leadership to achieve his incredible credentials.

Nearly Empty Leadership Benches

If we want to achieve, per Colin Powell, results beyond what management experts say is possible through positive leadership, you would expect to see an emphasis on developing our leaders and strengthening our leadership benches.

In May 2021, the Development Dimensions International (DDI) released results from a large study that surveyed 15,000 leaders and 2,100 human resource professionals from 1,740 organizations and 24 industries. Summarized by Edward Segal of Fortune magazine[3], this study provided key insights into the current state of leadership benches and presence across a broad spectrum. Of the organizations surveyed, only 11 percent indicated they had a strong leadership bench, the lowest observed level in 10 years. The DDI study illustrated that talent benches for leaders have a lot of opportunities for improvement. Clearly, we are not developing our people to be the leaders that fit Mr. Powell's definition, and therefore organizations are not elevated to the level of what is possible.

In January 2022, Goodhire, an employee screening service, shared results from a survey of 3,000 full-time workers[4] across 10 different industries about their relationship with their supervisors. Of the responders, 82 percent indicated they would quit their job because of a bad manager, illustrating the importance and the impact of a manager. On the topic of career development, only 32 percent indicated they felt their manager cared about the career progression of their team members. If only about one-third of responders sense their manager is supporting their development, and leadership benches are nearly empty, then we are failing to help people be their best. Ultimately teams and organizations are not achieving their full potential.

Significant Costs of High-Stress Workplaces

In addition to achieving the impossible, are there other benefits to positive leadership? In their 2015 *Harvard Business Review* article[5], authors Emma Seppala and Kim Cameron noted the financial impact of a stressful cutthroat culture on engagement. When looking at companies that operate in a high-stress environment:

- Work-related health care expenditures can be 50 percent higher. and employees have an increased risk of heart disease.

- There was a negative correlation between high-stress environments and worker engagement (high stress leading to lower engagement).

- In prolonged cutthroat environments, employees disengage, which is observed by feeling less valued, less secure, not supported, and not respected.

- Disengaged workers have 37 percent higher absenteeism, 49 percent more accidents, and 60 percent more errors and defects in their daily work.

- Higher-stress cutthroat companies experience higher rates of turnover, which leads to increased costs for recruiting and onboarding.

Additional insights from the American Institute of Stress confirm that workplaces have become overwhelmed by employees struggling with stress. Companies are eager to find ways to efficiently deal with this unfortunate truth. One cost-of-illness study estimated that "the cost of work-related stress ranged upward to $187 billion in the US alone."[6] A more inclusive analysis conducted by the American Institute of Stress found that after including factors such as absenteeism, turnover, diminished productivity, increased medical costs, and increased legal costs, the total economic impact of stress to US employers was estimated at $300 billion.

This shows the staggering impact of stress in the workplace and underlines the importance of leadership. If we put it crudely, challenging jobs combined with a toxic environment can be slowly killing employees. So ask yourself, do you want to work for years in a high-stress environment and then retire only to have a heart attack a few years later? It is a worst-case scenario, but clearly the cut-throat nature of old-school "command-and-control" organizations is not good for employees' health and the organization's productivity. Despite knowing for decades that positive work environments are better for employees, we have not been able to end the old-school practices. Many organizations still rely on a "results-only" focus to make supposed progress.

The Impact of Strong Company Culture

Ok, this is insightful data and impactful consequences, but what about financial performance related to positive cultures? Surely the old-school approaches must be more productive, and that is why companies still rely on those approaches for profits. Think again.

A year into the COVID-19 pandemic, Great Places to Work evaluated the impact of companies where the culture is highly rated (includes measuring whether people are able to reach their full human potential)[7]. This included a combined approach of researching companies highly rated by Great Places to Work and *Fortune Magazine*'s 100 Best Companies to work for. Using a "100 Best Index" including these strong culture companies, the stock performance in 2020 outperformed the broader market by 16.5 percent. You may ask, was this one year an anomaly? Using an annually adjusted 100 Best Index going back to 1998 revealed a cumulative return of 1,709 percent to Jan 2021 compared to the 526 percent return with the 3,000 largest US companies (also known as the Russell 3000 Index).

Yes, that is a 3.23-times higher return for companies with great cultures.

Our Changing Motivation to Work

Great culture and positive leadership can be healthier for employees and increase productivity, but what motivates people to work? From Monday through Friday, why do we get up? Yes, we need to provide financially for ourselves and our families, and we haven't yet figured out how robots can do all the work for us (someday, someday…). If we are only working to collect a paycheck, the days are long, and the hours are numerous. The reality is we do not want to just collect a paycheck; we want to do meaningful work and be part of an organization that has an impact greater than ourselves. Consider this: one-third of your life is spent at work. The average person will spend 90,000 hours at work over a lifetime[8]. Why not make them meaningful and impactful?

In a 2016 study related to goals or objectives by generation[9], a team surveyed 1,700 US workers from different generations. They asked responders to indicate what they were looking for when they are applying for a new job. The top four criteria for baby boomers (people born from 1946 to 1964) were as follows:

1. Quality of manager

2. Quality of management

3. Interest in type of work

4. Overall compensation

For millennials (born between 1981 and 1996), the top four criteria ranked for a new job were as follows:

1. Opportunity to learn and grow

2. Quality of manager

3. Quality of management

4. Interest in type of work

Even more recently, in LiveCareer's 2024 Different Generations in the Workplace Study[10], they found Generation Z employees (born between 1997 to 2012) took the prioritization of importance even further.

- 95 percent of Gen Zers want to do a meaningful job that goes beyond making ends meet.

- 71 percent of Gen Z workers would even cut their pay to do meaningful work.

What *motivates* people to work is changing. If employers do not adapt and focus on the importance and meaning of their work, they may be missing out on great talent.

With this, we see the strong need to prioritize and develop positive leaders. With the right focused structure, these leaders become inspirational examples that can exceed companies' financial performance, elevate organizational productivity, and most importantly, deliver employee happiness.

SUMMARY

- We've seen that positive leadership can make the improbable probable and the impossible possible.

- Leadership benches at large companies are not robust.

- There is cost avoidance and greater financial gains in positive healthy cultures, driven by positive leaders and leadership.

- Employees are more engaged and healthier in a positive leadership environment.

- There is a generational shift in the motivation for work: from older generations' value of a quality manager and management to younger generations who are looking for purpose and meaning from their careers.

We had one persistent fundamental question that needed an answer:

When people say "leader," what do they mean?

CHAPTER 2

What Is a Leader?

"You manage things; you lead people."
—Rear Admiral Grace Murray Hopper

"What is a leader?" appears to be a simple question. From our experience, we have been working 20-plus years to identify the answer to these four words. Not surprisingly, if you ask twenty people what it means to be a "leader," you will likely get twenty different answers. In countless job interviews, one-to-one meetings, and informational discussions, we asked people why they want to be a supervisor or manager. The common responses we heard included the following:

"I want to tell people what to do."

"I have good ideas and want people to follow them."

"I want to help people."

"I would like to make more money."

"It seems like the logical next step."

"I enjoy developing people."

"I want more responsibilities."

"I want to make more of an impact."

We have heard many versions of the above responses. Fundamentally though, the responses suggest people are not aligned on what it means to *be* a leader. If we are unable to agree on the definition of *leader*, then how can we develop positive impactful leaders, let alone inspirational leaders who can make the improbable possible. Adding to murky waters, there was also a common theme in the responses for people who wanted to be first-time supervisors or managers: titles indicating they were not responsible for leading a group of people. According to titles, they may have been team leads, analysts of different levels, or individual contributors, but they were not leaders. For those wanting to have a title signifying you are a leader, it's like you are on the outside of the "Leadership Club" looking to get in but not sure how entry works. This then begs the question: should the definition of a leader include those who don't have direct reports? (More on that in a bit.)

Browsing online for definitions makes it even more confusing. If you search for "leader," you will find the following definition from Oxford Languages: "the person who leads or commands a group, organization, or country."[11] Does this mean that leaders are controlling and commanding? Or ask yourself, Would you be motivated to follow someone because they *command* a group?

Neither would we. John C Maxwell refers to this as *positional leadership*, the lowest level of leadership, where we have to follow a supervisor simply because they are the boss, not because we want to follow them or even like them. (Likeability plays a role in what Maxwell defines as level 2 leadership[12].) This lowest level of leadership also generates the lowest level of productivity from people.

Still, we weren't satisfied. Something did not add up. People wanted to be leaders even though it appeared they were not aligned on the definition. In our effort to make sense of these findings, we needed to understand how people define *leader* and describe the qualities of a good leader. These questions sparked us to start our own study with a few short polls and then a more detailed survey on enjoyable and productive workgroups. We will share the detailed results of our research when we introduce you to the Enluma Leadership Model. Our first poll helps to understand who can be a leader. We asked close to 500 people, "When you think of a leader, which of the following best aligns with how you define a "leader"?

(A) Senior executive (CEO, VP, etc.)

(B) Team supervisor or manager

(C) Expert or highly skilled coworker

(D) Anyone, including myself

Thinking for a moment, how would you answer the question?

Articles about business leadership commonly focus on the C-suites or senior positions. One could then assume that a leader is only a senior leader of a company. Based on this observation, before we started our poll, our assumption was that the vast majority of responders would select options A or B. This aligns with the definition of a leader in any online search. This also aligns with the title-based hierarchy where only leaders have direct reports. However, we were surprised that the results went in a different direction.

We asked close to 500 people, "When you think of a leader, which of the following best aligns with how you define a "leader?" As depicted in the table, the feedback was very clear and the direct opposite of what we expected.

Who aligns with "leader"	Score
Anyone, including myself	77.5%
Expert or highly skilled coworker	10.7%
Team supervisor or manager	8.6%
Senior executive (CEO, VP, etc.)	3.3%

In thinking about this, this data illustrates a more modern definition of a leader, a definition more focused on impact as opposed to having control or a specific title or position. Additionally, multiple survey participants shared insightful feedback:

"Leadership is a quality, not a title."

"Leading is a choice that anyone is able to make. It is what sets people apart."

"Leadership is to develop, guide, inspire, and teach others, so they can help others do the same."

The survey results and the additional feedback point to a destination of helping others improve regardless of a position or a title. With these insights, we scoured resources looking for one definition that concisely encapsulated what it means to be a leader. Ironically, as we continued research to clearly define *leader*, we repeatedly returned to a 150-year-old definition that distills the very essence of leadership into a simple yet complex statement. (Thank you to the Bob Chapman leadership institute for initially sharing this definition.) The sixth president of the United States, John Quincy Adams, said of leadership:

"If your actions *inspire* others to dream more, learn more, do more, and become more, you are a leader."

If this is your first time reading this quote, please feel free to read it a few times. These nineteen words are a lot to take in. This is a dense definition, so let us unpack the key points together:

- Nowhere in Adams's quote does it say to command or guide others.

- Also absent is a position of authority. You don't need people reporting directly to you to help them to become more.

- One subtle inference is time. To inspire someone to dream more and become more implies the action is not quick. You don't become "more" overnight.

- One important assumption is about positivity. If you are going to lead someone to dream or become more, it's logical to assume this is through positive interactions.

- There is no exclusivity in this definition. In alignment with our poll results and our experiences, the definition indicates any-one has the capabilities and capacity to inspire others. Anyone can be a leader.

Serendipitously, this definition also concisely describes inspirational leadership. Yes, we kind of fell into that one. And we are glad we did. You may be wondering what we mean by *inspiration*. Similar to defining a leader, people's definitions of *inspiration* are not consistent. We see two types of inspirational leadership: one with short-term impact and one with longer-term impactful results.

Imagine a rousing half-time speech by a coach that turns around a team or when employees hear directly from a customer or patient on the positive impact of their work. These are examples of short-term inspirational leadership with immediate impact. Do they inspire people to be more motivated? Absolutely. But hearing the same speech every day for thirty days is not likely to have prolonged inspiring effects. With repetition, the same inspirational speech becomes less impactful, less inspirational.

On the other hand, with sustained inspirational leadership, people are happy to work hard now and into the future, resulting in increased engagement and long-term impacts. Let's take you back to our introduction, to Mr. Gurysh and the two basketball coaches who inspired the class and team, respectively, to do more and become more. Although they approached leadership with some similarities, their approaches were different. The fundamental result was the same: groups happily worked hard to achieve a lofty goal, a goal that at first did not seem possible. These leaders inspired us over a longer period of time, well beyond our time together. Based on our experience, our research, and existing data, you have likely experienced inspirational leadership and these positive and productive workgroups at some point in your personal or professional life.

To illustrate this, let's do a quick exercise.

Think about someone in your life who you respect and who had a positive impact on your life. This person, who could be a family member, friend, coworker, boss, or person you've read about, inspired you to dream more, learn more, do more, and become more. Can you name someone who helped you to be better?

Based on our data and experience, you can very likely name at least one person. The point is that we have all likely experienced inspirational leadership but may not have known it at the time. Most people have teachers, mentors, supervisors, family members, coworkers, or others who have helped them or inspired them to be better. That's also the surprising part of all of this. Inspirational leaders we can learn from, who help us grow and in turn, will develop others to be inspirational, are often hiding in plain sight. We may not have recognized them as inspirational leaders.

Our data and experiences indicate that while people experience inspirational leadership in professional contexts, they are rare and usually only appear in pockets within the organization. In other words, we see free-range inspirational leadership.

Returning to our initial list of "nagging" questions, let's mark an initial completion.

- **When people say "leader," what do they mean?**

  We now have an aligned definition for not just a leader, but for an inspirational leader. From John Quincy Adams: "If your actions inspire others to dream more, learn more, do more, and become more, then you're an *inspirational* leader.

- **Why don't we have a model enabling the development of inspirational leaders?**

- **What are the key elements of inspirational leadership?**

- **How can we more intentionally develop leaders who energize and inspire?**

- **Why don't we expect that every group and role is successful, fulfilling, and enjoyable?**

--------------------------------- SUMMARY ---------------------------------

- We concluded that leadership is an action of helping others and not a role or title and that everyone has the capacity to be a leader.

- In evaluating the definition of leadership, we reviewed an over 150-year-old definition of leadership that is inspiring and gives insights on achieving the improbable.

- With the John Quincy Adams definition of leadership, nearly everyone has experienced an inspirational leader; we just didn't know what to call them.

- Inspirational leaders are all around us. We have all seen or experienced them, but we must understand why they are rare in the business environment.

Next, let's explore inspirational leadership and understand why no existing model can effectively deliver it.

Why don't we have a model enabling the development of inspirational leaders?

PART 2

The Enluma
Leadership Model

CHAPTER 3

Introduction to the Enluma Leadership Model

"The only safe ship in a storm is leadership."
—Faye Wattleton

Every quarter, the US Bureau of Labor Statistics releases productivity reports measuring the number of hours worked compared to the units of output, and the United States is not alone in monitoring productivity. The Organization of Economic Cooperation and Development (OECD; based out of Brussels, Belgium) also compares productivity rates for countries all over the world. For over a century, these reports have focused on the output of the industries:

Revenue or Units Produced / Hours Worked = Productivity

Productivity metrics are intended more for manufacturing of units or common repetitive tasks and may not reflect what really is going on in our modern workplaces. In a recent Deloitte study[13], most of the global productivity growth has been in decline since the 1960s and since about 2010 for China.

Today's workforce is going through a new Industrial Revolution with increasing levels of automation, as more jobs focus on problem-solving and instead of the completion of common or repetitive tasks. This may explain why productivity has been nearly stagnant for decades. Ironically, even though our workplace is changing, most leaders surveyed indicated they are under more pressure to produce more with less. With quarterly stock targets and business reports, pressure is constant and highly focused on short-term goals (often targets <12 months).

Further illustrating the disconnect, employees indicate this antiquated approach focusing on productivity does not work. Instead, we see that employees are more highly motivated by human outcomes such as (1) what they achieve, (2) the quality and impact of their work, and (3) their growth and development opportunities. In the Deloitte report, they gave an example of a company that is taking a different perspective than the classical view of productivity: Hitachi. In 2020, Hitachi shared results of a company experiment where they shifted focus to employee satisfaction and happiness. What results did they observe? Profits increased by 10 percent. In what are typically challenging environments, call center sales per hour increased by 34 percent and retail sales by 15 percent. Hitachi is taking it further by using Artificial Intelligence (AI) to measure and predict employee happiness.

What the productivity data, workplace evolution, and the Hitachi transformation tells us is that high-stress environments where we push the immediate short-term result (focused on productivity and decreasing costs) without investing the time and energy for employees to be more effective, is at best marginally increasing productivity. From our own experience, we directly encountered that a high-stress "old-school" approach increased the rate of mistakes, challenged work-life balance, and in some cases caused health issues of employees. Unfortunately, leaders who solely focus on productivity and don't support employee effectiveness are likely to burn through people to meet their objective(s). These leaders may see a small short-term gain and a significant long-term loss.

Is there a better way—a more sustainable approach to achieve strong results *and* help people enjoy their work? An approach focused on challenging individuals, teams, and organizations by building tailored development plans (more on that later) and then measuring the impact on improved business results. Considering inspirational leadership, what role can a leader play to enable strong results?

To answer this question, let's revisit two elements of the John Quincy Adams definition of leadership, when your actions inspire others to *do more* and *become more*. It led us down a few conceptual avenues of thinking:

- An inspirational leader should help people in a positive way, not through fear or intimidation.

- Short-term, forceful focus on doing more with less does not lead to sustainable "productivity" improvements.

With this background, we were wondering how people could experience inspirational leaders throughout their career. If people are doing more and becoming more in a positive manner, then you would expect the result would be a productive and enjoyable team. People would be both motivated and would enjoy working hard. To explore these points, we designed several questions to better understand these inspiration-driven teams:

- Does everyone experience these workgroups? If yes, how frequently do people experience these groups during their career?

- Which behaviors of the leader and group create the positive and productive experience?

- What motivates people to put in the extra effort?

- Who is most likely to inspire or positively influence the team?

Leveraging these questions, we conducted a study to dig into understanding the drivers of these positive and productive workgroups.

We surveyed over 400 people from a variety of backgrounds. (Demographic data is in the Appendix.) We then wanted to compare our results to established literature on high-performing teams and the qualities of exceptional leadership, which constitutes the ideal mix of inspirational leadership. With high-performing teams, there may or may not be an element of inspiration, but we wanted to see how our results compared to established studies. These comparisons helped us to give context to our initial findings.

Before we started the study, we made three assumptions: (1) the occurrence of these workgroups would be rare (less than 50 percent of participants); (2) the positive nature and hard work would be largely driven by people's immediate supervisors (setting the tone); and (3) the key behaviors would be clear communication and effectiveness.

We found the results both surprising and insightful.

Of the people we surveyed, 90 percent responded "yes" to having experienced these productive and positive workgroups—much higher than we had initially expected. The number of times people experienced such a working group also took a surprising turn.

Of those who responded "yes" to a positive workgroup, the weighted average of the number of times they experienced these workgroups in their career was 4.8 times. We were absolutely surprised it reached a score of 4.8.

Think about it this way: across a 90,000-work hour career, assuming each role is three years long, then a person would be in an inspirational group on average for 28,800 hours or 32 percent of their career. This means the vast majority of working hours would not be guided by inspirational leaders who can help us reach our full potential.

To better understand who was driving the productive and positive experiences, we also asked people to rank the following groups and people on their impact of the positive experience (1 = most impactful to 4 = least impactful). Below are the results:

Group	Impact on positive experience
Our peers or workgroup	1.85
Our direct supervisor	2.37
Yourself	2.42
Managers or leaders above your direct supervisor	3.37

Much like the game of golf, the lower the score the better. In this case, peers or workgroups were more impactful than a direct supervisor or yourself. However, leaders above your supervisor or manager had the lowest impact.

Initial Findings

These positive and productive work groups occurred more frequently than we initially thought. Given these groups occurred more often because of yourself, peers, or direct supervisor, and less likely from senior leaders suggests that these groups are occurring randomly based on the people in the workgroup and/or the leader in charge. This can be described as *free-range inspirational leadership*.

We also wanted to understand what motivated people to work hard in the workgroup. Of the respondents who indicated they had experienced a positive and productive workgroup, the following were the three highest responses:

Basis for working hard	% of participants
Meaningful purpose/impact of the group	30%
Desire to see team succeed	28%
Care for others: "didn't want to let them down"	14%

The next question focused on behaviors. Specifically we asked, "What are the behaviors of the leader or group that drove the positive and productive experience?"

With this question, we used a free text field that could be completed by respondents. With the responses, we then looked for common themes in their response. Four primary behavioral elements rose to the top. These behaviors occurred at random without intentionality.

But what if we were intentional?

What if we expected and encouraged each of these behaviors?

What if these elements became part of the norm in how we operate?

The Four Elements of Inspirational Leadership

Based on our findings, we identified four elements of inspirational leadership.

- **Team First:** Create a "We before Me" culture

- **Accelerate:** Empower through Communication and Insights

- **Elevate:** Grow and Develop Together

- **Realize:** Achieve a Powerful Destination

Team First	Accelerate	Elevate	Realize
Create a "We Before Me" Culture	Empower Through Communication and Insights	Grow and Develop Together	Achieve a Powerful Destination

We'll take a closer look at these four elements in more detail in the next chapter, and we'll show how these fit into the full Enluma Leadership Model.

The Name of the Model

Combining the insights of our research survey with our experiences leading people and organizations, we wanted to ensure the model would serve as a framework for being an inspirational leader. The model needed to guide for action and not be a summary of theoretical approaches for inspirational leadership. Additionally, we challenged ourselves to meet two primary objectives with the model.

1. **Enlighten.** Provide a clear picture of what it means to be an inspirational leader.

2. **Illuminate.** Show the path to becoming an inspirational leader.

When these two objectives are combined, you get the "Enluma" Leadership Model.

The Role of Questions

As you'll see here in Part 2 as we introduce the Enluma Leadership Model and later in Part 3 where we guide you through application of the model, questions play an important role.

The importance of curiosity-based questions. We want to show that all leadership is enhanced through the use of curiosity-based questions. These questions can be a very powerful resource in any leader's toolbox.

As a leader, people will look to you for guidance and direction. For better or for worse, people see that you are in charge of the project, team, or organization. The challenge is unlike the academy award winning movie, you cannot be Everything, Everywhere, All at Once. In other words, as leaders we cannot and will not have all the answers. This is where you must rely on the team, the expertise they have, what they bring to the table every day, and together, the team will see the bigger picture.

This may sound counter intuitive, but the way to help the team feel empowered and to increase accountability, is through *questions based in curiosity*. In her book, *Change Your Questions, Change Your Life*, Marilee Adams[14] talks about how coming from a "Learner" mentality where you are asking questions to understand and being curious will help engage and motivate team members. Conversely, if you are coming from a place of trying to catch people doing something wrong, or as Adams puts it, a "Judger" mentality, the questions can spiral into a negative direction for yourself and others. People will see quickly that you are trying to catch them or assuming they screwed up. It goes back to how you see yourself and how you see others (more on this in Chapter 5).

Similarly to Marilee Adams, in the bestselling book *The Coaching Habit*[15], Michael Bungay-Stanier shares how questions can be the key to energizing an individual or team. Bungay-Stanier talks about a variety of types of questions that can help with coaching and feedback. For example, utilizing questions to engage the team, including:

"What do I (or you) really want?"

"What do you think is holding you/us back?"

"What is possible?"

You can see that these questions are not judging others but rather coming from a place of curiosity and to learn. The goal with these types of questions is to trigger thought and action from the individual and the team. With these questions, we energize people to come up with their own solutions.

Enluma Experience: Chris

In 2019, I (Chris) was coaching a team member (we will call him Bob) who was debating options on a path forward for an IT project (yes, there were many IT projects). Utilizing this approach, I asked Bob "What do you think is the best approach?" Bob gave two options, and then I followed up with, "What is your gut telling you?" Bob was leaning toward one approach for a few valid reasons. Bob then said he really appreciated the feedback and input that I gave him. This was hilarious because I only asked a few questions, and he already had a plan. He just wanted me to validate his idea. This discussion also helped Bob's confidence because in the future, he knew I was going to ask him his thoughts and ideas.

There is another powerful component of curiosity-based questions. If I'm asking another person "what they think" or in the case of Bob's example above, "what he thought was the best approach?", I'm showing that I respect and trust the other person. I trust that you are experienced. I trust that you know what you're doing. I trust you will do a proper evaluation and determine the right answer. As a leader, if you treat others as peers (even if they report to you), this can be a powerful tool. Just think if the vice president, director, business owner, project leader, or managers treats you like a peer, they are immediately showing you respect and trust. In turn, this will likely energize a team member because then they will not want to let you down because you treated them as a peer.

How questions can activate your leadership journey. Our intention with this book is to be practical and to make it easily applicable, so you walk away with a clear plan. A key method we are leveraging to ensure practicality is through the use of questions. As you will see later in the book when we discuss the model and its application within each leadership layer (more on those later), we leverage powerful questions to challenge you and encourage you into action. With questions, they cause an immediate laser focus in our brains. For example, if we were to ask you,

What did you have for lunch yesterday? Take a minute and think about what you had for lunch yesterday.

Something interesting just happened when you thought about that question. In most cases, your mind is now laser focused on the question and finding the answer. It's difficult to think about anything else. Your engagement just significantly increased. Physiologically, your brain has triggered the classic fight or flight response. Hundreds of thousands of years ago, we needed to quickly determine if the obstacle or challenge in front of us was safe or not. Similarly, your brain is quickly evaluating the social impact of the question.

It is safe to answer the question = I know the answer to the question, and I will look good (receive a hit of dopamine, positive reinforcement).

It's not safe to answer = not sure or don't know the answer and I think I will look bad (fight or flight mechanism for safety).

On the other hand, what happens if someone tells you what to do or gives you an answer. You may or may not be engaged. You could also be in your mental "happy" place or thinking about what is for dinner tonight or any plans for the weekend.

Enluma Experience: Chris

In 2018, I was presenting in an All-Employee Meeting for a team of about 300. During the presentation, I shared that a new Information Technology (IT) system was going to be launched in October of that year. I was looking directly at one team member who was also looking at me when I shared the timing of the project. Our eyes were locked. The next day, that same team member came up to me and asked, "Hey Chris, when are we launching that new IT system?". I didn't blame him, he was receiving a lec-ture (given the answer) and could have been off in his mental happy place. I also didn't know what was going on in his life and he may have had challenges or issues at home that were dominat-ing his life. But the point is, we can tune out lectures or speeches and our mind will wander, but questions, especially from a place of curiosity, will engage and energize. Questions from a place of curiosity help others to be part of the solution. Questions will activate people to focus on their personal journey, how they will grow as an inspirational leader.

By using curiosity-based questions, we wanted to show our readers we respect and empower you to take action. We also want you to really challenge yourself and think about the leader you want to be. In other words, when you retire and look back on your career, do you want to look back and see that you inspired others to dream more, learn more, do more, and become more?

SUMMARY

- Measuring worker productivity is no longer applicable for a large portion of the modern workforce, as they are not completing repetitive tasks.

- We surveyed over 400 people to understand the prevalence of productive and positive workgroups. Of those surveyed 90 percent had experienced these workgroups.

- We identified four elements of inspirational leadership:

  o **Team First:** Create a "We before Me" culture

  o **Accelerate:** Empower through Communication and Insights

- o **Elevate:** Grow and Develop Together

- o **Realize:** Achieve a Powerful Destination

- To enable the model, we will leverage questions to activate participants to focus on their journey. Throughout, we'll provide challenging questions to self-reflect and better understand the leader you want to be.

- Any leader can leverage the power of questions to both focus teams and elevate team members in both a respectful and challenging way.

CHAPTER 4

Inspirational Leadership Elements

"Nobody cares how much you know until they know you care."

—Theodore Roosevelt

The previous chapter summarized our research identifying the characteristics of inspirational leaders who led positive and productive workgroups. We noted that 90 percent of the respondents had encountered these workgroups, which led us to the four elements of an inspirational leader:

- **Team First:** Create a "We before Me" culture

- **Accelerate:** Empower through Communications and Insights

- **Elevate:** Grow and Develop Together

- **Realize:** Achieve a Powerful Destination

With these four elements, we did not want to rely on our study. We wanted to test our findings against respected literature to determine whether we were heading in the right direction or needed to refine the model.

Let's explore the four elements as an initial roadmap for becoming an inspirational leader.

Team First: Create a "We before Me" Culture

Meaning. It's critical to understand and focus on the collective success of the team. If the team is successful, then the team members will be successful as well.

Insights from study participants. Here's what some of the participants shared in their study responses:

- "I believe my team's openness and positivity was a huge factor. A willingness to see other perspectives and realizing our team has a wealth of knowledge was incredible to witness. This motivated me to want to contribute to the best of my abilities and showcase my knowledge as well."

- "I didn't want to let my team down. I also wanted to be the best I could be for them and for myself."

- "We respected each other. More importantly our manager respected us and would be 'in the trenches' with us."

- "Pride in my work output and helping the whole group function well, so we can all succeed"

- "Helping each other regardless"

Comparing our findings to key research. Our findings were validated by the below literature:

- In *The Leadership Challenge* by (James Kouzes and Barry Posner)[16], the authors list five practices of exemplary leaders. The second practice described is to "Inspire a Shared Vision," in particular, to enlist the team in a common vision and shared aspirations. This practice enables the team to be part of creating and owning the vision. The team is creating something bigger than themselves.

- Within *The Wisdom of Teams* by Jon Katzenbach and Douglas Smith[17], teams are the key performance unit for addressing and overcoming bigger challenges, not individuals working separately.

Our thoughts on Team First. In hindsight, this behavior seems logical for the success of the team, but at the time we did not see this one coming. If you flip our concise definition of this behavior (we before me) to "me before we," you can see how the group will be limited. A Team First attitude also illustrates a degree of humility and self-awareness that team members and leaders need to have. Sometimes, our existing processes, such as when we revert to individualism during annual reviews, don't help with the Team First approach and may significantly hinder team performance. On the positive side, if we prioritize the success of the collective, and the team knows it, each person will be motivated to not let the team down. This is feedback we heard multiple times from participants.

A Valuable Lesson for a Strong Team First Approach: Responsibilities versus Importance

If you have the opportunity to be a people leader, inevitably there is a challenge: people will want things from you. Team members will seek your approval for promotions, to join project teams, for financial approvals, for good performance reviews. Like it or not, people are going to want things from you. But here is the challenge; it's easy to mistake your responsibilities for people stroking your ego or indicating you're more important than they are. People will come to you for approval and requests. The reality is many people will come to you because of your title or role and not because of who you are as a person. But is that how you want to operate, and more importantly, is that how you want to be remembered?

So, what is at risk here? Ultimately, your long-term joy. If you lose your humility, then you will also risk losing the ability to openly talk to people within the same team or organization. Humility and the ability to talk with all people as if they were peers (and not subordinates) is a powerful tool of an inspirational leader. The Dalai Lama is the spiritual leader of millions of Buddhists (and non-Buddhists) throughout the world. In his classic book *The Art of Happiness*[18], he responds to the question around his importance or position in the world. His holiness's response, "I am just one of the seven billion people on the planet." In other words, he is not more or less important than anyone else.

For any leader, it's easy to think that we are more important than others because they are coming to us for input or approval. In reality, we may have more responsibilities and (this is why we are paid more), but we are not more or less important than anyone else in our organization. This may be a tough pill to swallow because of higher salaries and bigger titles. In most businesses, we can outsource almost the entire team. If the team is outsourced, they likely don't need you. After being promoted, getting a bigger salary and title, leveling your importance with everyone else can be difficult. However, thinking of yourself as one of the seven billion or one of the team, is also liberating. As a leader, seeing yourself as part of the team (not the most important person) changes your perspective and the resulting questions.

If you see yourself as more important, then you ask questions like these:

- Where is <u>my</u> request?

- How can <u>I</u> drive the team to raise the bar?

- How can the team organize around <u>me</u>?

- How can I get the most out of my team?

- What information or updates do I need?

On the other hand, if you see yourself as a member of the team (not more important), you ask team-focused questions:

- What is impacting the team's ability to deliver?

- How can we improve (including myself) and how can I help the team?

- How can we work around the team?

- How can we help the team to be their best?

- What information or updates does the team need?

You may also see a trend in the above lists that we illustrated in this chapter. Any leader needs to be careful with the use of two words, *I* and *my* versus using *we* and *our*.

Accelerate: Empower through Communication and Insights

Meaning. People will be set up for success when they have the information they need, including clear expectations on what good looks like.

Insights from study participants. Here's what some of the participants shared in their study responses:

- "Constantly communicating"

- "Frequent meetings and feedback, sharing detailed plans and follow-ups, honest and clear communication"

- "Seeking to understand various perspectives"

- "Everyone was open to giving and receiving feedback, with open mindedness toward the best decision regardless of who presented the idea."

- "We all kept in touch with each other, making sure to understand where everyone was at and what we needed."

Comparing our findings to key research. Our findings were validated by the below literature:

- In 2016, *New York Times* writer Charles Duhigg summarized the findings from Google's Project Aristotle[19]. The goal of the project was to understand why some teams at Google were more effective than others. Teams composed of individuals with advanced degrees and strong individual performance did not correlate to high-performing teams. The key driver for success of high-performing teams at Google was psychological safety, the ability to readily and freely share information within the team.

- For high-performing teams, Anita Williams Woolley and colleagues looked to quantify the collective intelligence of a team[20] by defining and measuring the characteristics of team performance. They found that the collective intelligence of the team was significantly higher when there was equal sharing of information within a team and no one person dominated conversations (evidence of emotional awareness).

- Taking these two a step further, collective intelligence can be maximized by utilizing inclusive collaboration and open communication[21]. In healthcare settings (such as hospitals), where people are encouraged and expected to collaborate and communicate, critical information leading to better patient outcomes is more likely to be shared, enabling the team to make better decisions and achieve improved patient outcomes by everyone having a more comprehensive view.

Our thoughts on Accelerate. This sounds logical and straightforward, but then why did we not see 100 percent of our respondents immediately mention the importance of readily sharing information. We likely need to look at communication in a different way. What if we looked at information or data as a commodity, like money?

Let's pretend that you work for a large manufacturing company. You're responsible for shipping and receiving, and another group handles the manufacturing. How would this company function if all of the finances for improvements or fixing issues were held by the manufacturing group, and the shipping/receiving group had little to no budget? The company would run the risk of building up inventory and couldn't get products to customers/distributors. What if we thought of information/data in the same way? If people don't have the information they need, then they will be limited in their potential. If you factor in a lack of psychological safety, then team members would not be creative and would have decreased problem-solving skills. Work, projects, or improvements would be delayed (if completed at all) because the data commodity would not be flowing to accelerate the team.

Elevate: Grow and Develop Together

Meaning. More than building relationships, team members actively look for ways to help each other to be better in order to make the team better.

Insights from study participants. Here's what some of the participants shared in their study responses:

- "Caring for each other; wanting success as a group"

- "The whole team had each other's backs. It didn't feel like we were alone."

- "Trying to help each other be better; zero competition within the group; focus on the group and not myself (attitude); instilled by each other, not the leader or administration."

- "Forgiveness, patience, [and] excitement for others' achievements"

- "High interpersonal standards of excellence, high interpersonal care, and great humor"

- "Allowing others to feel safe; supporting each team member; allowing each team member to contribute ideas without judgment"

Comparing our findings to key research. Our findings were validated by the below literature:

- Of the five practices of exceptional leadership in *The Leadership Challenge*[16], the fourth and fifth practices of (4) Enable others to act and (5) Encourage the heart, both speak to the importance of the power of helping others be better. For "Enable others to act," the two subparts to the practice include (i) foster collaboration through building trust and facilitating relationships and (ii) strengthen others by increasing self-determination and developing competence. In particular with collaboration, Kouzes and Posner explained, "Without a feeling that 'we're all in this together,' it's nearly impossible to create the conditions for positive teamwork." For "Encourage the Heart," the focus is really around positive reinforcement (recognition and celebrating values). This includes nurturing and helping team members grow to be their best. The authors also shared that their cases of strong human connections produced spectacular results. If these strong connections result in having fun on the job, then this can lower turnover and enhance problem-solving skills, creativity, and morale.

- One of the "uncommonsense" findings in *The Wisdom of Teams*[17] is that high-performing teams are not common because they require a high degree of personal commitment to one another and must have partnerships with each other. This may sound intense, but the commitment to improve others directly correlates to helping each other be successful.

Our thoughts on Elevate. At first, this behavior may sound "soft," but it illustrates a fundamental point. We can all grow and learn along while facing challenges and difficulties. If a leader demonstrates through words and actions that they are looking out for a team member and truly care, then this will reduce the perceived barrier within the team to challenge each other and further increase the overall psychological safety. The goal is to help all team members be their best, and the most effective way to achieve this is to support them. This does not mean to ignore individual performance issues; on the contrary. Even in the fifth practice within *The Leadership Challenge* of Encourage the Heart, Kouzes and Posner talk about the importance of addressing performance issues for the betterment of the team. This also does not mean we abandon goals or objectives in favor of "fluff" or "soft" stuff. The underlying goal remains the same: to help people be successful to achieve (or potentially exceed) the objectives. Collectively though, this all goes back to helping each team member be their best, so the team can be its best.

We'll discuss this more in the coming chapters, but helping a team member be better isn't limited to helping others. It includes helping and leading yourself. If you're focused and invested in your own growth, you're more likely to be energized to help others because you see the benefit and value. Also, if you lead yourself with empathy and compassion, you're more likely to use the same approach with others. Leading yourself first may seem contradictory, but it's key for helping others.

Realize: Achieve a Powerful Destination

Meaning. The positive and productive workgroups were not just working together for the sake of working. They were completing something meaningful or significant, in short, helping to make a better future.

Insights from study participants. Here's what some of the participants shared in their study responses:

- "The entire team's desire to achieve a goal never before obtained by the company"

- "The team dynamic; everyone was actively engaged in improving things; there was a shared common goal; lots of humor and camaraderie"

- "Hard work; a common goal; respect and a commitment to doing the best possible job we could"

- "Wanting to keep putting more onto your plate for the sake of the goal"

- "All for one team; cooperation; working for the same mission/ vision"

Comparing our findings to key research. Our findings were validated by the below literature:

- With Project Aristotle[19], two of the five core attributes of high-performing teams were (1) the meaning to the work, and (2) the resulting impact. If the goal of the team is meaningful and can make a significant impact, this will drive the team to be more effective.

- Within *The Wisdom of Teams*[17], the reason a team is assembled is to address a performance challenge or needed outcome. A meaningful challenge can further galvanize the team around the impact of their work.

- In *The Leadership Challenge*[16], the third practice of "Challenging the Process" illustrates the importance of "generating small wins" to unlock the opportunities and gain momentum. It's easier for teams to work hard if they are making progress.

Our thoughts on Realize. Meaningful execution, with a clear positive goal, means we are progressing an action or improvement that has never been achieved before or will have a significant impact. It's not about being effective for the sake of being effective; it's about progress toward a better future. The goal is for everyone on the team to know the destination and to enable them to be effective.

This ties to the "big why" for the team. If people don't know "the why" then they are less likely to engage and less likely to be inspired. Think back to when you were young. If your parents asked you to clean your room, you likely asked, "Why do I need to clean my room?" If your parents responded, "Because I said so," then you likely reluctantly cleaned your room and didn't do a good job (if at all). In contrast, if your parents shared, "Because we have company coming" or "Because we are trying to sell the house and we need it to be clean," then you're more likely to have done a better job. Granted if you were like many kids, you started to clean your room, forgot, and then had to be reminded. Joking aside, making solid progress and then realizing a meaningful goal (the "why") is a powerful combination. Others will know you are serious about moving forward, and you're building strong momentum.

The Interplay of the Four Elements

Given an inspirational leader represents the intersection of a high-performing group and a strong leader, our hypothesis is that the ideal spot in the diagram below is the center gray intersection where all four elements overlap. To challenge this, we then wondered what happens if one of the four elements of the Enluma Leadership Model is removed. Can the experience still be as productive and positive?

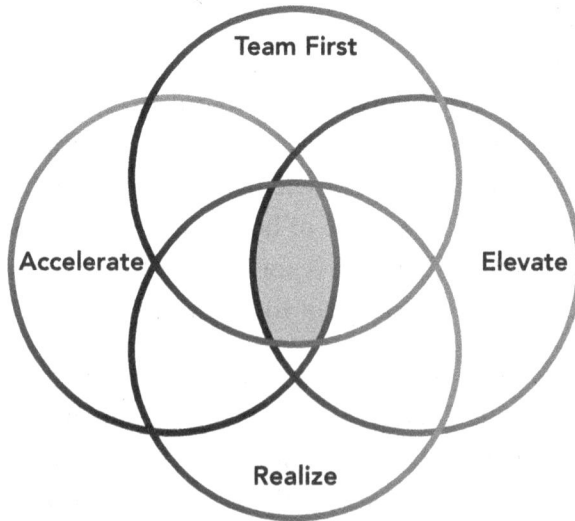

Team First: Create a "We before Me" culture

If people take credit for a team's work or start blaming others when there are issues (me before we), then the team will have problems. Morale will drop along with motivation and effectiveness. Unfortunately, we can all likely remember a fellow team member or direct supervisor who took credit for our work or the work of the team. It is demotivating. The power is in the collective team, not the individual.

Accelerate: Empower through Communication and Insights

If people don't have the information they need due to poor communication or lack of psychological safety, people will be limited in their ability to make decisions and take action. Utilizing the example of collective intelligence and psychological safety in healthcare, critical information held by a few people on a team is less likely to be shared, limiting the team and potential patient outcomes. Also, if team members do not feel safe to speak up (low psychological safety), sharing of information can be delayed or "softened" for team members due to fear, thus prolonging making decisions or taking actions.

Another aspect of needed data and insights relates to the individual and team expectations. If you don't know what is expected of you, it will be difficult to meet let alone exceed expectations. People will then work toward what they think is the right direction and will be at risk of diverging from the overall organizational vision or goals. Winning as a team or individual will be more difficult.

Elevate: Grow and Develop Together

At the start of Chapter 3, we explained how the approach for global productivity and the push for doing more with less is out of touch with today's workforce. This ties back to the old school "command-and-control" mentality where we see people simply as resources to get things done and not people who have opportunities and challenges. Combined with results-only approaches, we risk decreased engagement and increased error rates and absenteeism. In other words, if caring and helping others to grow is removed, the data suggests the team will be less effective and less motivated. People will see quickly that leaders or fellow team members don't care about their well-being and development, and are focused solely on achieving the result. Also, the leader or team member is likely to sacrifice the team for either their personal betterment or to achieve the result. Either way, not good.

Realize: Achieve a Powerful Destination

Logically, if you are not effective, then you lose credibility, and people lose motivation. Even if you take the time to define a meaningful goal (better future) but don't make any progress, the team loses momentum (a dangerous combination). For this element of the Enluma Leadership Model, we must consider what happens when you don't have it, we also need to consider what happens when effectiveness or achieving the result becomes the only behavior (removing the other three). Effectiveness, productivity, or "getting things done" is what most businesses ultimately look toward. Did we achieve our profits? Did we complete the project on time? Did we produce the projected number of units at the assigned time? If you only focus on effectiveness or productivity without a meaningful goal, you'll establish some superficial credibility ("we get things done"), but it may feel like the team is working hard to sort deck chairs on the Titanic before it hits the iceberg. You're effective but unlikely to fully realize the future. The team will not be bought in and will not have full engagement beyond doing what they need to do in order to get a decent annual review (and keep getting paid). Short-term gains are completed to achieve a goal, but in the long term the ship is sinking.

This also may sound familiar to the old-school cultures we have described. With only looking at the output, the temptation of leaders is to "get the most out of your people" and quite often, "do more with less." An aggressive, results-only culture can risk decreasing engagement, decreasing team members' output, increasing the rate of mistakes, and higher absenteeism. This is the irony. An overly aggressive culture laser-focused on results without providing the support and resources to make the team more effective and not clearly communicating where the team/organization is going (meaningful goal) is very likely encouraging and enabling mediocrity.

Let that sink in.

Focusing only on results and timelines and not supporting the team through good communication, sufficient resources and tools, and a team-first attitude, prevents teams from more effectively reaching their goals, especially over the long term. If you only focus on productivity or the output and don't move to more modern ways of measuring worker performance in a world that is more focused on troubleshooting and diverse work than repetitive tasks, you will miss significant opportunities. Herein lies the opportunity with the Enluma Leadership Model.

--- SUMMARY ---

- We looked to intentionally test the four elements observed in the positive and productive workgroups.

  o **Team First:** Create a "We before Me" culture

  o **Accelerate:** Empower through Communication and Insights

  o **Elevate:** Grow and Develop Together

  o **Realize:** Achieve a Powerful Destination

With these four elements tested against prominent literature, we further reinforced the Enluma Leadership Model.

CHAPTER 5

Leadership Layers and the Combined Enluma Leadership Model

"There are three essentials to leadership: humility, clarity, and courage."

—Chan Master Fuchan Yuan

In Chapter 2, our data combined with the John Quincy Adams definition of leadership, illustrated that anyone, regardless of position or title has the potential to be a leader. We all can positively impact another person. With this understanding and alignment, we wondered who is most likely to inspire you to help you be your best.

As a next part of our research, we asked close to 450 people the following question:

Throughout your career, who has been most likely to motivate you and help you be your best?

A. Your direct manager or supervisor

B. Your peers or coworkers

C. Yourself

D. Executive leaders (above your manager or supervisor)

Take a moment and think how would you answer the question? As with our previous poll, the results were surprising.

Who is most likely to motivate you	Score
Your direct manager/supervisor	33.9%
Yourself	34.5%
Your peers or coworkers	25.1%
Executive leaders	6.5%

The people most likely to motivate and help you be your best are your immediate supervisor or managers, and/or yourself followed closely by your peers or coworkers. A CEO, business owner, or a senior leader in the organization, likely multiple layers removed, is least likely to motivate you. While we were initially surprised, upon further reflection in a lot of ways this makes sense. Why? These are people with whom you interact the least on a daily basis. This is also consistent with the question in our broader survey on who was most likely to impact the positive and productive workgroups.

As we thought about this further based on our experience, the way we impact or influence a peer is different than a direct report or when leading an organization with multiple reporting levels. There certainly are common themes, but the approaches are different. Each of us can influence others, but how we inspire and help others to be their best differs based on the layer of leadership. Let's explore those now.

Layers of Leadership: Additive or Separate

The journey to becoming a great inspirational leader is a progression to strengthen and align all three layers: Foundational Leadership, People Leadership, and Organizational Leadership.

The layer that everyone regardless of role or position must consider (and master) is Foundational Leadership, the base upon which the other layers are built. First priority is self-awareness and understanding how we control and understand ourselves. To be most impactful to everyone (regardless of their role or position) each individual should strive to improve their Foundational Leadership.

If you are promoted and have the opportunity to lead a direct team, you can seek to build your People Leadership while you continue to demonstrate Foundational Leadership.

Finally, if you earn the opportunity to lead multiple levels of people and demonstrate your Organizational Leadership, you continue to leverage the Foundational Leadership and People Leadership fundamentals. You do not transition from layer to layer; you add layers to your leadership capabilities, starting with the Foundational Leadership layer.

Foundational Leadership

For many, the concept of leading peers and in particular yourself may come as something that has not crossed your mind. If you think about it, everybody has peers. And who do you spend all of your time with? Yourself. One of the most challenging aspects in any role is the dynamic of leading peers, since you have no direct authority. As you move up in an organization, you may encounter more challenging personalities because egos tend to grow with added responsibilities. This is especially true in hierarchical organizations where senior roles are difficult to obtain and can be challenging to keep[22]. Let's explore leading yourself and peers in more detail.

Leading Yourself

First, how you lead peers or others, all starts with how *you lead and perceive yourself.* To expand on this includes the following:

- Emotional intelligence

- Self-perception

- Self-compassion

Emotional Intelligence. Over the past twenty years, the concept and importance of emotional intelligence in the workplace has steadily grown. To align on the definition[23,24], emotional intelligence is the ability to recognize and reason about your own and other's emotions. This includes the ability to control one's emotions and correctly apply them to everyday tasks.

As noted by Dr. Bhavana Arora, these are "essential skills identified for a good leader...as being able to control impulses, to curb impatience, to properly regulate mood and to prevent frustration, ...and to have empathy and hope." A person who is calm and focused under pressure enables the broader team's success by role modeling strong behaviors, and also likely has high emotional intelligence.

Exploring this concept a little further, Dr. Arora notes the five key elements of emotional intelligence:

- Self-awareness: understanding and recognizing your emotions and your strengths and weaknesses including supporting your decision-making

- Self-regulation: managing your emotions and mastering the ability to show and utilize restraint and control your emotions

- Motivation: your drive to improve and achieve, setting high standards for yourself and working consistently towards your goal, commonly coincides with optimism

- Empathy: important skill to put yourself in someone else's shoes and sense how people are feeling and doing

- People skills: also known as a "people person," which connects to your social skills and the ability to deal with others or in summary by understanding your emotions, also understanding how you respond to other people's emotions

When you look at this list, the importance and impact of emotional intelligence on leading yourself and others becomes quickly apparent. This is further illustrated by visualizing a person with low emotional intelligence (low EQ). A person with low EQ would not control their emotions, have questionable motivations, and likely "bulldoze" people—not someone you would want to work with or, more importantly, work for. Fundamentally, this illustrates the importance of emotional intelligence and its connection to the ability to lead peers and ourselves

Self-perception. In addition to emotional intelligence, another aspect of Foundational Leadership is self-perception, or how you see yourself. This theory, first popularized by Dr. Daryl Bem[25], indicates that through our own behaviors we better understand our own motives and attitudes. If you are easily angered, you start to see yourself as an angry person and assume in the future you are likely to get angry again. Similarly, if you have been successful under pressure in the past or focused on positive aspects in the past, you're likely to be successful and positive under pressure in the future.

Why is this important? There are two reasons. First, how you see yourself (positive or negative) is apparent to those around you. For example, if you have a negative opinion of yourself, your actions are likely to be negative (no surprise). The second reason is your self-perception impacts your view of others. If you're optimistic about your capabilities, you're more likely to be optimistic about others. Again, it all starts with how you see yourself and your actions.

Self-compassion. As we lead ourselves and others, the concept of self-compassion dovetails nicely with self-perception. Self-compassion is largely defined as having three components[26]:

- Being kind and understanding to oneself in instances of suffering or perceived inadequacy

- A broader awareness that all people will struggle and have challenges, which are part of a shared human experience

- An awareness of one's emotions and the ability to face self-doubt and negative feelings

Self-compassion is a view that if I make mistakes, I can learn from them in order to avoid making the mistake again. Note that the goal is not perfection but a more healthy and powerful focus on continuous improvement.

There's another important benefit of self-compassion. Individuals who exhibit self-compassion are seen to have improved social connectedness and satisfaction, with decreased anxiety, depression, and neurotic perfectionism[27]. Ironically, what is the most common dysfunctional behavior observed at the senior executive level? Pathological narcissism[17]. Narcissism is more likely to be observed in individuals showing excessive levels of self-esteem. We'll discuss this later, but excessive self-esteem or arrogance can lead you to think and believe your ideas and direction are better than anyone else in the organization. Elevated self-compassion is aligned with a focus on learning and continuous improvement—great traits and goals for any layer of leadership.

Combining the three elements together—emotional intelligence, self-perception, and self-compassion—can enable powerful behaviors to lead ourselves and others. Sustainable approaches for leading yourself or others include empathy with a strong focus on continuous improvement.

Leading Your Peers

Let's now explore the other side of Foundational Leadership: *leading peers*, the ability to impact our peers or others where we do not have direct authority. As we introduced earlier, our ability to lead ourselves impacts how we lead others. You may wonder, "What impact can one person have on their peers?" For example, can negative interactions between two people have a lasting impact? In their *Harvard Business Review* article[28], authors Christine Porath and Christine Pearson evaluated the impact of incivilities (rude behaviors) in the workplace and their impact on coworkers. Of the 800 workers surveyed, examples of incivilities included yelling at others, making stinging or biting jokes, or other negative behaviors. Among the workers who were on the receiving end of incivilities:

- 48 percent intentionally decreased their work effort.

- 47 percent intentionally decreased the time spent at work.

- 38 percent intentionally decreased the quality of their work.

- 80 percent lost work time worrying about the incident.

- 63 percent lost work time avoiding the offender.

- 66 percent said that their performance declined.

- 78 percent said that their commitment to the organization declined.

- 12 percent said that they left their job because of the uncivil treatment.

- 25 percent admitted to taking their frustrations out on customers.

This data illustrates that one person's regular bad behaviors can have a significant impact on those around us. Magnifying this perspective, imagine if these results were consistent across the global workforce of billions of people. That is a huge loss in personal satisfaction and happiness at work along with countless hours of lost output. In other words, individuals may cause a toxic environment pulling others down.

In addition, Porath and Pearson surveyed 244 customers who observed incivilities from employees in restaurants and shops. Consumers who observed incivilities were more likely to leave or turn away. The authors also noted a study, where consumers entered a simulated bank and observed a representative publicly reprimanded another employee. Of the participants who observed the incivility directly, only 20 percent said they would continue to utilize this bank as compared to 80 percent who did not observe the incivility. Our behaviors have the potential to not only impact those directly around us but can negatively or positively impact potential customers and clients.

If leaders don't work on emotional intelligence and don't have a healthy perception of themselves or self-compassion, then how can they lead other people or organizations? Over 20-plus years, we have had the opportunity and challenge to lead other people in a variety of roles. As we progressed in our careers, people commonly asked us what we look for in others to identify whether they are a good candidate for a people leader role. We consider four questions:

1. How do they manage their time?

2. How do they manage their words?

3. How do they manage their emotions?

4. Do they care about others and the team?

If these sound like they directly correlate to emotional intelligence, self-perception, and self-compassion, you are right. These Foundational Leadership skills are critical for people leaders with direct reports. Do you want to work with someone who spends too long on tasks or not enough time? Conversely, do you want to work with someone who is unpredictable, leaving you constantly wondering what they will say or how they will act? If one of your peers does not care, you know it and likely try to avoid working with that person. Unfortunately, we probably all have worked with people in the past who did not manage their time, words, and emotions well. From our experience, it is exhausting.

This is why the Foundational Leadership is the base upon which the other layers are built. This first layer is truly the base that enables People Leadership and Organizational Leadership. It all starts with how we lead and perceive ourselves.

People Leadership

When most people think of leadership, the classic example is people leadership. The scope of work can be anything, and the leader facilitates the team with day-to-day challenges and may work in the trenches. People leadership is not for everyone but can be the most challenging and rewarding parts of a person's career.

Thinking back over the last 25 years, it is hard to recall the awards we have received. However, if you ask us about the specific people we have helped coach and develop, we could start listing the people on whom we have made a positive impact. This is ultimately the impact and responsibility of a people leader. Processes can be improved, and businesses can be revised. Once you leave that role or job, processes can unravel, and businesses can stall. However, the impact on the people you had the opportunity to lead as direct reports can last far after you have left the role.

Similar to the circle of influence described in the classic *7 Habits of Highly Effective People*[29], people leaders have circles of impact that must be considered and are likely to stretch beyond Foundational Leadership.

All people leaders impact direct reports as well as family and friends of the direct reports. A good example: if you've had a job where you were not happy, Sunday afternoons are frustrating because you do not want to go to work on Monday. When you are not happy, your family and friends also see and feel it, and it may dominate the dinner table conversations. *They are impacted.* Conversely, if you enjoy and like your job, you actually look forward to going to work on Monday. So, the "Sunday Afternoon Effect" applies both ways and illustrates the impact of People Leadership.

Enluma Experience: Chris

In 2022, I (Chris) reconnected with a former team member (we'll call her Tina) who was on a team I led from 2016 to 2018. It was a call center, and these jobs were not easy. Our call agents had to speak with frustrated customers working to understand their financial options for different products. Tina asked me if I remembered a specific discussion we had in 2017. I didn't immediately recall because that team was quite large (160 people), and I'd tried to interact with as many of the team members as possible to get their input/feedback. Tina shared that we had discussed project management and her interest in becoming a project manager. Tina shared that I'd suggested that she get involved in informational technology (IT) projects as we had many and they offered quick experience. I had also recommended that she work to get certified as a project management professional (PMP). The combination of the experience and certification could potentially help. From this brief conversation a few years ago, Tina took my advice. She got into a few IT projects and signed up for and completed her PMP certification. Then she developed as a project manager and eventually led larger IT system launches. She shared that I had given her a plan that helped her grow and develop. From the tone in her voice, I could sense it had been a positive change. This is the lasting impact of inspiring People Leadership. Even after I had moved on from the role, Tina was still growing and developing. I didn't remember the original discussion in

2017 but will never forget our discussion in 2022. This illustrates a key goal of People Leadership: helping direct reports (direct teams) be their best (more on that later).

Enluma Experience: Jan

In 2018, I led a global organization with locations in Europe and the US. Merging the organization into a global structure was a recent change that presented cultural and organizational challenges. Development of my team and employees was always top priority, so to better understand the organizational and cultural challenges, I moved one employee from Germany to the US and one from the US to Germany – each for six months. The individual who moved to Germany, let's call him John, is who I want to highlight to demonstrate the impact you have as a leader. Before his move to Germany, we clearly laid out the expectations for John, provided a structure for check-ins, and ensured he had all the tools and resources to make this assignment successful. His assignment was successful, but I did not anticipate what happened next. John decided to stay in Germany, and he changed his career to writing children's books. Years later I asked him what made him successful, and his response was insightful and personally rewarding. He told me that my leadership, support, coaching, and showing him what was possible were the reasons he took on his business venture. To this date, he still lives in Germany and has successfully created a series of children's books. I am proud of the lasting impact I had on his personal and professional life.

Organizational Leadership

When a leader is multiple levels removed from the people doing the day-to-day work, this is where Organizational Leadership comes into play. In this environment, the leader is more involved in the strategy or longer-term planning for a team and less in the day-to-day operational execution. The organizational leader must helicopter in and out on key issues as they occur. Organizational Leadership also has a broader impact on the culture of the team. With an organizational leader role, the impact of your decisions and actions increases. Similar to the People Leadership layer, your circle of influence is even larger because there are more people in the organization you have the opportunity to lead. Yes, a potential bigger "Sunday Afternoon Effect," which means if you are a poor organizational leader, you can ruin a lot of people's Sundays. These actions and decisions will rely on direct reports (most likely people leaders) and partnership with peers (Foundational Leadership) to be successful. A truly effective organizational leader will not and cannot operate in a vacuum.

Herein lies the importance of the layers. We concluded that if you have strong Foundational Leadership, you have high emotional intelligence, a healthy self-perception, and a level of appropriate self-compassion for yourself and your peers. We determined that if you have strong People Leadership, you want to help your direct team be their best and see them grow and develop. Strong Foundational Leadership enables better People Leadership. Leveraging the strengths of Foundational Leadership and People Leadership, as the organizational leader you want to create and develop an organization with a strong future direction and healthy culture, a culture where people can be successful and voice their opinions or disagreements and a future direction that people understand and want to be part of. The success of the organization is the top priority. All leadership layers working together have a synergistic effect that is greater than the sum of their parts.

As we noted in the previous chapters, organizations with toxic cultures decrease engagement, impact productivity, and increase turnover and absenteeism. It is highly likely that innovation and rapid problem-solving will be compromised and instead replaced with complicated in-office politics, self-preservation, and fear of upsetting the boss(es). Additionally, if the team doesn't know where they are going, then it's like being on a road trip without a destination: fun at times perhaps but ultimately uncertain and frustrating. In the end a lot of effort is spent, but you may not get anywhere. Combining a toxic culture with a team with an unknown destination is a recipe for mediocrity (at best). This is the impact and responsibility of Organizational Leadership. It's not easy, but getting it right is rewarding.

John Quincy Adams Definition and the Connection to the Three Layers

To help define an inspirational leader, we are utilizing the definition from John Quincy Adams:

> "If your actions inspire others to dream more, learn more, do more, and become more, then you're an (inspirational) leader."

When considering the three leadership layers, the initial layer that connects best is the People Leadership layer. Logically, helping the direct team be their best falls well within the definition. But what about the other two layers, Foundational Leadership and Organizational Leadership? Let's think a minute about the elements of Foundational Leadership with high emotional intelligence, positive self-perception, and self-compassion. All of these steer toward helping others and helping yourself. Our research illustrated a key aspect of positive and productive workgroups, which was team members looking to help each other to make each other better.

A result of the Foundational Leadership Layer is to inspire your peers to dream more and become more, all starting with how you lead yourself and make your dreams become a reality.

Now let's apply the same thought process to the Organizational Leadership layer. This layer is focused on inspiring the organization to dream more, learn more, and do more, together. Later in the book we will expand on the two primary goals of Organizational Leadership: (1) Establish and foster a positive and open culture where people can thrive and excel and (2) Determine and communicate where the organization is going. Leveraging this approach will not only align and mobilize the team, but also show everyone throughout the organization how to achieve incredible results that fuel organizations and grow people. Organizational Leadership will inspire short-term success and sustainable results (do more) through the creation of more inspirational leaders (become more).

Although the approach for inspirational leadership is different, all three layers align to and support the John Quincy Adams definition.

Combining the Model Elements and Leadership Layers

In this section of the book, we have summarized our polls and study results which led to the identification of the four elements of the Enluma Leadership Model:

- **Team First:** Create a "We before Me" culture

- **Accelerate:** Empower through Communication and Insights

- **Elevate:** Grow and Develop Together

- **Realize:** Achieve a Powerful Destination

These four elements were the most prevalent in our study and illustrated the core elements of an inspirational leader. Then in this chapter, we noted how we inspire and lead others is additive and considers if you are leading yourself, peers, direct team members, or an organization. The three layers of Foundational Leadership (yourself and peers), People Leadership (direct team), and Organizational Leadership (multiple levels of influence) combine together. Strong skills and development in each layer will enable and elevate the other layers, and Foundational Leadership is the base for future success.

Now taking the four elements plus the three leadership layers, the Enluma Leadership Model starts to take shape:

	Team First Create a "We Before Me" Culture	Accelerate Empower Through Communication and Insights	Elevate Grow and Develop Together	Realize Achieve a Powerful Destination
Organizational Leadership				
People Leadership				
Foundational Leadership				

There is another aspect we briefly touched on in Chapter 2: the notion of those without direct reports on the outside of the "Leadership Club" looking in. With the Enluma Leadership Model, everyone has the potential to be a leader. Nobody is on the outside looking in. This also means everyone has clear expectations of strong Foundational Leadership. If expectations are clear for everyone, it is easier to gauge who is ready for the People Leadership layer by assessing the strength of their Foundational Leadership because it all starts with Foundational Leadership.

The same applies for understanding the strength of a team member's People Leadership to determine whether they are ready for an Organizational Leadership opportunity. This illustrates another aspect of the additive nature of the layers, a clearer career progression.

Foundational Leadership ⟹ People Leadership ⟹ Organizational Leadership

Team members have clearer expectations that can enhance individual readiness for the next layer through purposeful development planning.

Starting in Chapter 7, we'll further explore and define the intersections in the model. Each intersection has a theme and questions to help guide and activate you. The combination of the themes and questions will help to progress your journey to grow as an inspirational leader and enable you to then develop others around you.

—————————— SUMMARY ——————————

A leader is not just a person with a direct team. Anyone can positively impact another to learn more, dream more, do more, and become more. This includes how we lead ourselves and peers without direct authority through Foundational Leadership.

- The Foundational Leadership layer is based on high emotional intelligence, a positive self-perception, and strong self-compassion. These behaviors enhance leading yourself and peers and support continuous improvement and resilience.

- The next layer, People Leadership, is where you have direct responsibility for and impact on others. The fundamental goal is to help direct team members be their best.

- The third and last layer is Organizational Leadership. In a role that is multiple levels away from the team doing the day-to-day work, you are now more responsible for the strategy and direction of the team along with setting the culture and tone to realize the future state.

- With the three leadership layers and the four elements the Enluma Leadership Model takes shape. It is a 3 x 4 matrix, with each intersection being a theme to work toward that will be activated through the power of questions.

CHAPTER 6

Leadership Glue

We described our initial observations related to those who are recipients of inspirational leadership. We have identified four key elements of inspirational leadership. For all four elements, there were two characteristics that kept coming up:

- Trust: a feeling of security, mutual respect, and open communication that enables people to work seamlessly and effectively together

- Fun: a positive, supportive work environment where employees feel valued and can enjoy their work

Ironically, these two were fifth and sixth in terms of most common elements behind our top four for inspirational leadership. If you don't have trust, the Enluma Leadership Model falls apart. And if you're not having fun, the work or environment becomes a grind. So, we see how these two elements serve as a kind of "glue" holding everything together. Now we'll dig a little deeper into each of these two elements of the glue.

Glue Element #1: Trust

"If you don't have trust inside your company, then you can't transfer it to your customers." —Roger Staubach

What do you know about trust?

We all have likely experienced the impact of working with people we trust:

- It is easier, less stressful.

- Information flows more freely.

- We trust that they will listen.

- We trust they will not overreact or yell at us.

- We trust they will follow through and get things done.

Why is it that some people trust more quickly than others? Not surprisingly, researchers have found that some people are more prone to immediately trusting someone. This is called *swift trust*[30], giving people the benefit of the doubt right from the start. In contrast, other people need time to gain insights and experiences of the person. This is called *knowledge-based trust*. Some people are more predisposed to swift trust than others. All people typically develop knowledge-based trust, albeit some people may take longer than others. Intuitively, swift trust is more fragile and likely to be broken.

Why do we bring this up?

Some people are inherently more likely to trust people initially or more readily. It is based on their personality and life experiences. Others simply take or need more time to trust others. When people are first joining a team, they are likely wanting to understand and experience the team dynamics and what are the hot buttons[31]. Most team members are likely to be quieter at first and less likely to challenge the team. The opportunity for an inspirational leader is to increase the trust of any new team member by making them feel heard, providing an opportunity for learning, and providing an open environment to ask questions. This includes prompting existing team members to create a similar environment.

Additional points to consider when building trust, we commonly are assessing people to see whether they are competent, have integrity, and are a kind person. This may not be controversial, but to build trust you need to get to know people and they need to get to know you. This will also help you understand the challenges they are going through and ideally, help understand why they act and do things the way they do.

Enluma Experience: Chris

A good place to start is with curiosity and empathy. With my first director role, I had the opportunity to lead a call center of about 150 team members who supported patients in better understanding their health insurance and coverage options. Already a complicated topic, most patients called in with many questions. On top of that, the team was divided by who they talked to (patients, doctors, or service providers), and the prior management expectation was for each team to focus on their individual area and not talk to the other group—in other words, work in silos. The patient-facing group didn't partner with the doctor-facing group who didn't partner with the service provider-facing group. Silos limited collaboration opportunities and isolated the teams. What do you think trust looked like? It goes without saying that the culture had a lot of opportunities for improvement.

So, what did we do?

We organized a listening campaign with the entire team. We did Gemba-walks, a management practice that originated from Lean manufacturing and the Toyota Production System. The term

Gemba is a Japanese word meaning "the real place" or "where value is created."[32] During a Gemba walk, managers and supervisors visit the workplace to observe processes, engage with employees, and understand the work being done. We shadowed team members while they handled calls and asked questions about the process. If you're not familiar with Gemba-walks, the goal is to map out the flow of the process and identify opportunities based on data and insights from team members. We also did multiple rounds of 1:1s with all 150 team members to gain feedback and insights about how things were going.

Here is the key part. We took action based on their feedback. With the process mapped out, we included analysts in the optimization to get their thoughts on what we could improve. Using the 1:1 infrastructure, we built a plan that we shared with the entire team to demonstrate we were listening and taking action.

If you have not completed an exercise like this, you might be very apprehensive and think that team members will ask for the world if you give them the opportunity. It is quite the opposite. If people do not know you, they are likely to first test you for small improvements. For example, I remember having a 1:1 with a team member, Kathy. At the end of the 1:1, I asked Kathy, "What is one thing you think I should do right now to help?" She didn't like that her name tag at her desk said "Kathleen" instead of "Kathy." Immediately after the 1:1, Kathy and I walked to our administrative coordinator and printed a new name card. For the next few weeks, every time I saw Kathy, she thanked me for making the change. Most importantly, as small as this change may seem, I was starting to build trust.

We also had team members who requested sit-stand desks because they would appreciate being able to stand while handling calls. With their feedback, we checked our budget and determined we would be able to support the request. Within a few weeks, multiple team members had sit-stand desks. Similar to the Kathy example, most team members were very appreciative.

This demonstrates the knowledge-based trust that takes time, especially for those teams with low morale and that have not had full support of leadership in the past. Building trust takes time and intentionality. The team needs proof and progress that shows you care and will help them.

Over the course of two years, we continued this listening campaign and took action. We saw a number of improvements. For a process that previously took weeks to a month to get a replacement medication to a patient, we shortened it to just days. The improvements were a result of understanding the process, listening and acting on feedback from the broader organization, and building trust to work with all team members. We also saw our culture scores go up significantly in annual surveys. What made me the most proud was helping dozens of people to improve their individual performance resulting in promotions or success in other roles across the organization. When I say "we," it was genuinely a team effort of our leadership team being aligned to help and challenge people to grow and be the best versions of themselves. The listening campaign with action was key to building knowledge-based trust, unlocking positive behaviors, and ultimately enabling our success.

Enluma Experience: Jan

Another example to mention is when I first took over a global cross-functional organization. The organization handled patients' critical information and was often on the critical path to get new products in the hands of customers. It was with one of these new products that we identified a mistake, a simple mistake but one that absolutely could not be on a physical product. The individual who made the mistake felt responsible and accountable, and she worried that this would be the end of her career at the company. Apparently, this was prior practice. We immediately corrected the mistake and quickly followed up with a thorough investigation.

This individual had been with the company for 23 years, all in the same area. I told her, "I trust that you know your process, so I really need you to lead the investigation, retrace your steps, and identify where this went wrong." As so often is the case, the failure was a process failure, not a human failure. She identified the process gap rather quickly. I made her part of the solution in fixing the gap, and she deployed this across the organization. There was no consequence to this mistake for the employee; we, the organization, had set her up to fail. Trusting (and empowering) employees to become part of the solution will gain trust in the leader, the organization, and ultimately themselves.

Seeing the Team as More Important than Yourself

In the three seasons of the acclaimed show Ted Lasso, the title character, an American Football coach in England, repeatedly demonstrates the importance of trust (at all layers). As an organizational leader of an English Premier league football (soccer) club AFC Richmond, you would think it would be all about him, but his focus truly was on helping his players and establishing a culture of respect and support for each other.

(We'll do our best not spoil the show for those of you who have not seen it.)

Near the end of season 1, the owner of the club Rebecca admits she has been purposely sabotaging Ted's every step along the way[32]. She wanted to sabotage Ted in order to destroy the team, the only thing her ex-husband Rupert truly ever loved. What does Ted do? He immediately forgives her. Ted was recently divorced and points out that divorce is difficult and can make you do crazy things. Ted shares that if you care about someone and have a little love in your heart, there isn't anything you can get through together. Most of us would have been furious with Rebecca. Instead, Ted utilized empathy and an apology as an opportunity to build trust and improve the relationship with Rebecca. It wasn't all about him.

In the last episode of season 2, Ted is exposed in the local newspapers for having a panic attack at the end of an earlier match[33], even though at the time he said it was stomach problems. Unfortunately, his players discovered Ted had lied to them. Illustrating self-compassion and a team first approach, Ted issues an apology to the players directly:

"..Every choice is a chance, fellas. And I didn't give myself a chance to build further trust with you. To quote the great UCLA college basketball coach John (Wooden) 'It is our choices, gentlemen, that show what we truly are, far more than our abilities,' Now I hope y'all can forgive me for what I've done. Cause I sure as heck wouldn't want any of you to hold anything back from me."

Ted uses his mistake as both an opportunity to build trust with the team and to teach. This showed both the vulnerability to admit he erred and the compassion to hope they would not hold anything back from him. Reading this quote, you can't help but wish you had a people or organizational leader who would be this honest. The players were treated like peers by the coach.

Glue Element #2: Fun

"If you're not having fun, you're doing something wrong."

—Groucho Marx

In the classic leadership book *The Leadership Challenge*, authors James Kouzes and Barry Posner[26] interviewed thousands of people about when they were at their best, in the authors' words, when they demonstrated exemplary leadership. In these thousands of interviews, two attributes were present in every single story of exemplary leadership: working hard and having fun. "Working hard" may not be a surprise, but are you surprised to see that "having fun" was integrated into every instance of exemplary leadership? So it begs the question: How is fun connected to inspiring leadership?

While too much fun can be a distraction and a model for failure, a workplace with no fun at all will have a direct impact on an organization's endurance and ability to achieve its deliverables. A balanced amount of fun is critical. Research has demonstrated that fun at work has a positive impact on employee engagement, creativity, performance, and sense of belonging, which all combined ultimately increases employee retention and development.

Fun and laughing specifically will also have great health benefits. It is proven that laughing makes us more resilient, reduces disease, and strengthens our immune system. So, if a company or department performance improves and there are health benefits, why do so few companies and leaders prioritize fun or a positive experience as part of their leadership strategy?

As we have mentioned in earlier chapters, the goal is to help others be their best. A study by Great Place to Work in 2023 summarizing data from over 1.1 million US employees across multiple generations[35] illustrated a direct connection between well-being and fun in the work environment. In their book *Work Made Fun Gets Done*, Dr. Bob Nelson and Mario Tamayo[36] looked to understand what exactly makes a job fun. In particular, they were looking to provide clear examples of exactly what managers and employees can both do to lighten the tone in the work environment and enable employees to have more fun at work. *Work Made Fun Gets Done* is a great resource for those trying to make the environment more fun. In short, it illustrates that fun (1) elevates productivity, (2) increases retention, (3) increases resilience, and (4) is required for high-performing teams.

From all of this, here is the key point: balanced fun or the right amount of fun is a secret sauce every business needs to better engage and motivate its employees today.

Enluma Experience: Jan

During my years as a leader of a global organization at a Fortune 100 company, we launched many new important products. The expectations were "launch in 24 hours" with the clock starting at regulatory approval. Launch in 24 hours often meant employees working until deep in the night and shuttling printer proofs to the supplier to confirm print feasibility. I stayed with the team during "launch nights," and unless there were management decisions, my role was essentially nonexistent. I realized however that introducing fun, such as group dinner at 7:00 p.m., an ice cream break at 10:00 p.m., or a candy snack at midnight positively impacted morale and motivation. Something simple to create an enjoyable break had a big impact. It provided moments for collaboration on the work done, laughter to lighten the mood, and connection to energize each other for the remaining work. With this team-first approach we never missed any timeline—quite an impressive accomplishment.

For most of us, a large portion of our day is spent at work. Often, you spend more of your waking hours at work and with colleagues than you do at home. Assuming an average working life span of 45 years, this means we will probably spend about 90,000 hours at work[7]. We may as well enjoy ourselves, right?

As a leader in any of the layers, you may be unsure about what you can do to make the work environment more fun. Here is the good news: you don't need to have all of the answers. The team already knows what can make work more enjoyable. To unlock the power of a positive or fun experience, the only thing you need to do is to tap into this by making it a priority.

Enluma Experience: Jan and Chris

In 2019, we met at a leadership event and quickly discovered a shared passion for leading teams and developing people. Our two organizations would not commonly engage with each other, even though we likely had team members who would be interested in working in the other area. We identified an opportunity for the teams to meet and connect. A collective team from both organizations planned a half day off-site team building to network, connect, and have fun. Team members from both organizations entered into a dessert bake-off, and then everyone voted for the winners. It did not cost much and had a positive impact. As part of winning, Chris got to throw pies at Jan's face. (Jan claims he's still trying to get the whipped cream out of his ears!) Most importantly, everyone enjoyed the time together, had a good opportunity to network with team members from another area, and enjoyed a welcome break from everyday work. It was a half a day investment of fun that resulted in lasting connections and positive cultural impact.

After reading the example, let's break down the connection to our leadership model. As organizational leaders, it truly was a minimal investment of time: prioritize fun, enable a cross-functional team, provide resources and a governance structure for questions and decisions. We chose and enabled the right team members to collaborate and meet people from the other organization, and the peer structure created fun and innovative ideas for team-building. The key takeaways here are as follows:

- Creating space for fun is not difficult.

- Employees are incredibly creative.

- Team members appreciate the break and sincere recognition from their leaders.

Having fun and a positive experience at work matters, and there is an important role for any leader to create an energizing environment. It begs to wonder what happens if your place of work, your leader, or your work group does not prioritize creating this environment? What is at stake if results are prioritized over creating a fun, energizing culture. In short, a lot is at stake. Let's explore this next.

The Cost of Unnecessary Drama

We've covered the value of fun and the impact it can have on individuals and an organization. On the opposite end of the spectrum, what is the cost of unnecessary drama or unconstructive conflict in an organization? In the CPP report[37] from 2008, the team surveyed 5,000 individuals from nine countries across Europe and the Americas to understand the frequency and impact of drama and unhealthy conflict in the workplace. Their key findings of the 5,000 individuals were as follows:

- 85% have to deal with conflict at work.

- On average, 2.1 hours a week are spent dealing with conflict.

Our guess is that you would much rather utilize 2.1 hours a week on increasing the energy and morale on a team and making progress toward a meaningful goal and not dealing with unhealthy conflict. In terms of the causes of the unhealthy conflict, the top three findings were warring egos, workplace stress, and heavy workloads. Unfortunately, 85 percent of respondents of the 5,000 individuals indicated they had to deal with unhealthy conflict (drama) at work. With those that dealt with unhealthy conflict, what were the primary impacts?

- 27 percent - conflict led to personal attacks

- 25 percent - conflicts result in sickness or absence

- 18 percent - people left the company

Looking at these impacts, the unhealthy conflict or unnecessary drama is likely to destroy the foundation of the team.

- 67 percent have gone out of their way to avoid a colleague because of a disagreement at work

- In the US experiencing unhealthy conflict is more prevalent among women, generally (71 percent, versus 64 percent of men)

The majority of people surveyed actually avoided colleagues. Now, we have all likely heard the justifications for unhealthy conflict, "I'm being hard on the team to challenge them," or, "What doesn't kill us makes us stronger." High expectations are good, and challenging a team is good. The question is how to challenge the team or individuals—in a healthy and sustainable way, or in a way that is likely to increase attrition, increase sickness, or lead to project failure. To put it another way, organizations commonly look for ways to increase their financial performance. One likely impactful approach, work to minimize unhealthy conflict and this could give people back up to two hours a week (or five percent of their time).

Now you likely noticed that the conflict noted above was designated as "unhealthy." If the team trusts each other and searches for ideal solutions, healthy conflict is likely to occur. Healthy conflict is like polishing a rough rock: the goal is to make improvements and make it better. Unhealthy conflict is more like shattering the same rock into multiple pieces, destroying it. As you work to define your journey toward being an inspirational leader, you'll notice healthy conflict is part of the process of continuous improvement.

With the addition of the Glue Elements, the Enluma Leadership Model continues to take shape.

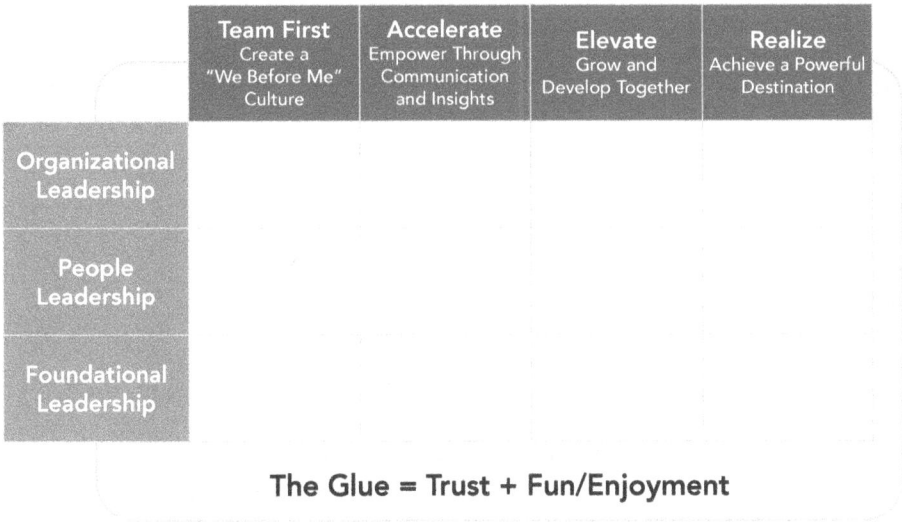

	Team First Create a "We Before Me" Culture	Accelerate Empower Through Communication and Insights	Elevate Grow and Develop Together	Realize Achieve a Powerful Destination
Organizational Leadership				
People Leadership				
Foundational Leadership				

The Glue = Trust + Fun/Enjoyment

──────────────── SUMMARY ────────────────

- We introduced the two elements of the glue for the Enluma Leadership Model: trust and fun.

- In defining trust, we looked at swift trust and knowledge-based trust and how different people develop trust. We also explored the importance of listening and then taking action based on team members' feedback to build trust.

- We also reviewed the opposite of trust—unnecessary drama and the high destructive cost of unhealthy conflict or drama.

- Team members are more likely to work harder if they work in a fun and enjoyable environment.

PART 3

The Enluma Leadership Model in Practice

CHAPTER 7

Foundational Leadership

"Everyone is a leader because everyone influences someone."

—John C Maxwell

Enluma Experience: Chris

In January 2013, a Fortune 100 company was spinning off a large division into a separate new company. As part of the separation, the newly formed company decided to move to a single company-wide enterprise resource planning (ERP) system. I had the opportunity to lead the deployment of the ERP system at the Manufacturing and Research and Development locations. I led a small team focused on change management, communication, and go-live project planning. This small team interacted with every impacted location/site and all functional groups including Manufacturing, Quality, Purchasing, Finance, Supply Chain, Customs, and many Information Technology (IT) groups. As a small team, we learned a challenging lesson on leading without authority across various teams and hundreds of people.

Ahead of joining the team, leadership had put in a lot of time planning the project with a clear meaningful goal (global alignment of the company's inventory management and finances) and established aggressive but achievable timelines because the project had sufficient resources and tools (relevant for our discussion when we get to the application of the Enluma Leadership Model for the Organizational Leadership Layer). Also important, leadership was very intentional with adding team members (including external consultants) that fit the desired culture of the team. It was clear that leadership wanted a team that would work well together and challenge each other to deliver the project successfully.

Challenges were in no short supply. Tough decisions were needed on the operating model and implementation for each location. Compounding this, the manufacturing sites were located in a variety of countries, and the teams supporting the go-lives were located around the world. Coordinating the go-lives, I had to learn quickly as I could barely spell ERP at the start of the project. I quickly built relationships with my peers that enabled open and honest discussions. Leadership held activities early on for the team to get to know and understand each other. Additionally, because I was not an expert in the content, I was in a constant mode of curiosity to learn from all team members. Each challenge was different and required our team to dig in, understand, and then develop a plan. Because the project was a global implementation, I was in a position where I had to understand all of the information and then propose a plan to leadership. To do this well required collecting information from a lot of people and connecting different areas and concepts, including previous, current, and future system launches.

During the project, when I shared with friends and family that I was leading the go-live efforts of an ERP project, the responses were consistent, "Oh, double the timelines," or, "You'll never finish that project on time." Family and friends shared stories of how they had been involved with ERP projects that took years longer than planned or were still ongoing.

Each go-live had its own challenges, but contrary to feedback from family and friends, all of the scheduled launches were completed on time. The planning and support were key to the success, as was the open and honest collaboration among peers. When issues or challenges occurred, we focused on evaluating solutions and paths forward (not blaming or finger pointing). We also sought out the best ideas and options, used laughter to manage stress, and genuinely looked out for each other. As a result, there was only limited complaining while regularly working six days a week for almost two years. This experience is also one of my positive and productive workgroups, despite it being around a highly complex ERP implementation.

This story illustrates the power of strong peer-to-peer collaboration (and leadership support, which we will get to in later chapters). In our surveys, we've seen peers are just as likely (if not more likely) to inspire you than your direct supervisor. Peers are especially more likely to inspire you than leaders above your immediate supervisor. Here is the challenge: we often do not think about powerful collaboration with our peers until we get into a cross-functional role, a people leader role, or an organizational leader role where the success is directly related to how peers partner together. As a result, the value of Foundational Leadership is often overlooked, underestimated, or implemented when it is too late.

For all team members in any organization, a significant opportunity exists to stress the importance of collaboration when they are individual contributors so this skill is inherent if they were to go on to become a people or organizational leader.

Before we explore implementation of the Enluma Leadership Model at the Foundational Leadership layer, let's ask ourselves some questions. Take your time to reflect and answer.

- Think of an issue that occurred in the last few months. (These issues can be non-work-related if you don't have a good work example.)

  o What was the issue, and how did you react to it?

  o How do you see yourself?

  o How hard were you on yourself?

  o What was effective about how you reacted?

  o What would you have changed or done differently?

- Imagine a similar issue occurs in the future.

  o How will you choose to react?

  o How would you like to view yourself?

- Similarly, think of a challenging situation/interaction with a peer (might be the same issue used above).

  o What made the situation or issue so challenging?

  o How did you interact with your peer?

  o How did your actions or behaviors impact the outcome of the interaction?

- Think about current or previous peers. Are most people easy to work with or more difficult? (This is not "get along with" but rather how productive you are with your peers.)

- Looking forward, what is the impact and type of collaboration you want to have with your peers?

Now, what is the value of these questions?

You need to consider the impact you want to have for a few reasons. The first reason is to better prepare you for challenges that will occur in the future. Days, months, or years from now, you may be in a tough situation where you question your abilities or you have a peer who is difficult to work with. By understanding your thoughts in advance, you can set expectations for yourself and for how you want to collaborate; otherwise, you run the risk of your behaviors being pulled down to the lowest common denominator. Anticipating challenges and your responses can instill mental resilience, enabling you to take the path that makes you proud.

The second reason is that life is frantic and constantly on the move. We're laser-focused on the task at hand, and it's tough to take time to think about the future or the impact we want to have. By thinking about the impacts you want to have, you have a yardstick to measure your future behaviors and ultimately, your remaining career. If you ask yourself these questions on a regular basis, the yardstick can and should evolve over time.

Our goal starting in this chapter is to illustrate *how* to be an inspirational leader through Foundational Leadership. To unlock the model, we will use the *power of questions*. As we mentioned in Chapter 3, questions stimulate areas of your mind that help you focus and drive action. They also illustrate whether you have the answers you need or if it is a question you need to work on. Questions also give you an effective way to channel your energy and control your thoughts. This is not meant to be a meditation or yoga session. The key is to control your thoughts, or you run the risk of your thoughts controlling you (without you knowing it). Consider these questions as starting points for your leadership journey. Over time, we encourage you to modify, remove, or add questions to help you implement the spirit of each theme. The goal is to reinforce and improve with each of the themes to become stronger in each layer.

Now for all three leadership layers, we are going to look at questions that help you from few different perspectives:

- Challenge your assumptions and viewpoints.

- Think about what is possible.

- Nudge you to action.

Team First: Create a "We before Me" culture

For Team First, we observed various insights from our survey responses:

- An attitude of openness and positivity

- Realizing the team has a wealth of knowledge

- Focus on the group and not myself; instilled by each other, not the leader or administration

- Not wanting to let the team down

- Respect for each other, knowing everyone would be in the trenches (if needed)

- A clear sense of team and how people fit into the goal

- Offering help and encouragement to team members when needed

- Shared goals and prioritizing the success of the team over personal accomplishments

Noting these insights, the resulting theme for Team First in the Foundational Leadership Layer:

Foundational Theme for Team-First: *Prioritize Shared Success*

With the theme of Prioritize Shared Success, the following questions can unlock great potential:

- Do you understand what your peers need in order to maximize collaboration (work more effectively together)?

- What does combined success look like for you and your peers? If your peers are successful, do you see that as you are then unsuccessful?

- Do you have open ways to discuss opportunities, issues, or challenges with peers? To provide easy ways to share information.

This list of questions is short and powerful. In old-school, command-and-control cultures, blaming (and even shaming) is very common. If the goal is clear and meaningful and the focus is on finding solutions, then teams will embrace issues and challenges and find a way forward. Additionally with a *Team-First* mentality, if one person is struggling, the entire team is struggling.

Accelerate: Empower through Communication and Insights

As we shared in Chapter 4, we received numerous insights around communications that enable. There were various common insights from our survey:

- Open and frequent communications by team members

- All ideas and feedback welcome

- Common goal and expectations to understand various perspectives

- An ambition to understand everyone's state of mind and what they needed

- Authority and ownership for decision-making across all team members

- Emphasis on the importance of active listening

With these insights, the Foundational layer theme for Accelerate:

Foundational Theme for Accelerate:
Communicate to Enable

From these insights, the following questions can unlock great potential:

- With a challenging situation, do you remain calm and set a tone of confidence and determination?

- With mistakes and issues, do you regularly look to understand the root cause and identify solutions, not cast blame?

- How do you integrate other ideas to balance or challenge your own ideas?

- During a day, how often do you request information versus give? (Hint: the goal is a balance of the two).

As noted in Chapter 4, if we conceptualize information as a commodity, the goal with the questions noted above is whether the team has the information or perspectives to be successful or whether you "value the information commodity." The questions also come from a point of curiosity to better understand the issues or challenges with the goal of sharing information across the team. It is critically important to note that whoever has the most information does not win. If team members and cross-functional staff don't have the information they need, then everyone loses. The goal is to enable whole-team success by sharing relevant insights and information.

In terms of the type of information needed, performance feedback is critical for yourself and team members. This is where there is a lot of overlap with the Team First and Elevate elements: Grow and Develop Together. And to make a connection to the Realize element as well, if the team is working toward a meaningful goal and you or a peer is struggling, the team is not performing optimally. Providing feedback or support to a peer or looking at your performance from a place of curiosity (such as, why am I or my peer struggling) will improve team interactions and result in better outcomes.

An additional consideration, different people need different degrees of intentionality to enable information sharing. If peers are co-located and talk multiple times a day, the barrier to sharing information is likely low. Teams that are located in different buildings, countries, or time zones, may benefit from an intentional approach to sharing information. The hallway conversations are not readily achievable. We also need to realize some people don't feel comfortable talking in groups, which could be a cultural or personal preference, so other options may be needed. The bottom line remains: understanding how different people communicate can readily increase the flow of information and power results.

Elevate: Grow and Develop Together

Similarly, below are key insights we observed from our survey responses:

- Caring for and helping each other

- No competition within the group

- Wanting success as a group

- Forgiveness and patience as key traits in the group

- Excitement for each other's achievements

- Infusion of humor

- Helping others to feel safe

With these insights, the Foundational layer theme for Elevate is:

Foundational Theme for Elevate: *We Are in This Together*

With the theme of We Are in This Together, the following questions can unlock great potential:

- Do you actively look for opportunities to help your peers improve?

- What is your approach to engaging challenging or difficult peers? Consider what *you* can do differently.

- How often are you connecting with peers to talk about life outside of work? In other words, how well do you know your peers?

With the above questions, the goal is to reinforce the notion of winning together. This is where self-compassion really comes in. We all know that mistakes happen, and we also grow by learning from mistakes. Understanding your peers' expectations, aspirations, and opinions ensures that the cohesive and connected team will improve.

Realize: Achieve a Powerful Destination

Below are insights we observed from our data:

- A desire to achieve a goal that either has never been completed before or has a significant positive impact

- The destination (or vision) understood by all and a level of excitement to pursue the destination

- Shared belief that the destination was worth pursuing

- Active engagement in improving things, with a shared common goal and lots of humor and camaraderie

With these insights, the Foundational layer theme for Realize is:

Foundational Theme for Realize: *Build Momentum*

With the theme of Build Momentum, the following questions can unlock great potential:

- What are your plans to build goals and momentum with your peers toward a destination or if a destination is not defined, toward improvements with your peers?

- Have you defined roadblocks to making progress (including short-term and longer-term roadblocks)?

- Do you discuss meaningful goals with your peers in a way that enables progress and building momentum?

With a clear meaningful goal, progress, even if small, is key. As a result, the theme is to build momentum. A meaningful goal without progress is a wish. And the goal is not to build a wish list of things we'd like to do, but rather a goal we want to and will achieve.

To summarize this chapter let's revisit our Enluma Leadership Model. We can now slowly see the 3 x 4 model is starting to fill in with the themes for each block of the Foundational Leadership layer.

	Team First Create a "We Before Me" Culture	Accelerate Empower Through Communication and Insights	Elevate Grow and Develop Together	Realize Achieve a Powerful Destination
Organizational Leadership				
People Leadership				
Foundational Leadership	Prioritize Shared Success	Communicate to Enable	Win Together	Build Momentum

The Glue = Trust + Fun/Enjoyment

---------------------------- SUMMARY ----------------------------

When you summarize and connect all themes, the overall goal for Foundational Leadership becomes apparent: to create an environment where everyone can perform at their best.

We now identified the themes for Foundational Leadership. To enable the Enluma Leadership Model with Foundational Leadership, we acknowledged:

- **Team First:** Prioritize Shared Success

- **Accelerate:** Communicate to Enable

- **Elevate:** We Are in This Together

- **Realize:** Build Momentum

  With these themes and the power of questions,

- The themes begin to provide an action plan for how you can develop as an inspirational leader through Foundational Leadership.

- We've provided an initial list of questions to support this development.

- We encourage you to adapt the questions and modify them, so they best support you in your journey.

- The questions will likely change with time and your growing experiences, which is good.

Last but not least, nothing is stopping you from using the questions today to start your inspirational leadership journey. Remember, application is a great step to building a habit.

CHAPTER 8

People Leadership

"To lead people, walk beside them. As for the best leaders, the people do not notice their existence ... When the best leader's work is done, the people say, 'We did it ourselves!'"

—Lao Tzu

Enluma Experience: Chris

With my first leadership role, I inherited an existing employee. We'll call her Barbara. This was an environmental health and safety organization, and Barbara's role was to scan paper copies of safety data sheets (documents that are shipped with chemicals) and save them to a shared drive all day long. That's all she did for about seven years. In our first 1:1, I asked Barbara, "So you scan safety data sheets all day and then store them on our website; I don't know how you don't go crazy." With more experience leading people, I would have known this was probably not the best approach. However, Barbara replied, "Yeah, it's terrible." Then she said something revealing. After working seven years with the company and having multiple bosses, this was the first time she had a 1:1 with her boss. I was disappointed in her previous managers, as they'd treated Barbara as someone not worth their time. With this insight, I asked a seemingly simple question, "Barbara, I understand your current role is not the most enjoyable, but what is it that you'd like to do?" With that, she perked up a bit and said that she was interested in building web pages.

Together, Barbara and I did some searching. There were no classes offered at our company, but a local community college offered them. Happily, Barbara took multiple classes and about nine months later was building websites for our team and other teams. Two magical things then happened. First and most important, Barbara was noticeably happier. She still completed her core work (now faster) and had time for the more enjoyable work. Second, people then told me how I did such a wonderful job with Barbara. All I did was ask Barbara what she wanted to do, get her into classes, and identify opportunities for her to build webpages, something teams needed anyway.

What does this story illustrate? Helping someone be their best is not always about dramatic transformation. Instead, it comes from a place of curiosity to better understand the person and then equally important, helping them to progress. Different people have different interests, and some may want to be a vice president someday and others may want to learn new skills for their current role. There are different degrees of ambition, and that is okay. Also, it's worth pointing out that this approach with Barbara was not about holding her accountable or making sure she got things done, but rather helping her. It didn't require that much time. Helping people be their best comes from a place of curiosity and genuine care. Another key point, we know that all people are more likely to be happy and engaged when they are learning and growing, especially if they are learning something that was their choice, their interest. The good news is direct reports know what they would like to learn and how they'd like to grow.

As a people leader you need to ask what you need to do for the direct report and the team to be successful? You can frame this in two ways: helping direct reports to be (1) the best versions of themself they want to be and/or (2) the best versions of themselves that others (including yourself) see. This is a key difference.

Not everyone is a rock star, and that is okay. Consistent steady performers are the backbone of every organization, but if someone can't deliver what is needed for the role, either the role is not a good fit for them, or they may not be a good fit for the team. What is the reason we bring this up? If you don't address one or a few underperforming employees, then the broader team may see it as acceptable to underperform or worse they will lose respect for the people leader (you). In other words, with difficult or underperforming direct reports, it's more important to think about the message you send to the broader team by inaction as opposed to the stress of managing the poor performer. Yes, managing an underperforming employee is exhausting (if they don't turn around their performance). We have both had to manage our share of difficult employees and unfortunately had to let people go. If you don't address the issues in a timely manner, you run the risk of losing the respect of the team, making it more difficult to be an inspirational leader.

With this, let's look at some questions related to People Leadership. In all cases, we are asking about the direct team members who report to you.

- As a people leader, think about recent difficult situations or projects where you worked with one member of the direct team to make progress or resolve the issue. In detail, describe how you interacted with the direct team member(s). (Note, if you don't have direct reports, do the same exercise where

you worked on an issue with your immediate supervisor/
manager.)

- What did you like about the interactions and why?

- What would you have done differently and why? If your answer
  is "nothing" or "not much," what opportunities to improve
  could you be missing or overlooking? (Hint: If you have the
  opportunity to lead a direct team, there are always areas to
  improve.)

- Thinking forward in the future:

  o How would you like to act or behave differently in address-
    ing issues or challenges to get to your ideal leadership
    approach?

  o How would you like to inspire direct team members?

Focusing on leading a direct team, here are a few tougher questions:

- As a people leader, why would anyone want to be led by you?

- Do you know the short-term and long-term career interests of
  each direct team member?

- Are you helping them toward their aspirations? Do you believe
  they can get there? If not, how can you help or challenge them?

These are tough questions that require emotional awareness to
understand your strengths and your limitations as a people leader (ties
into Foundational leadership). When we think about people leaders,
there is an inherent meaningful goal within this layer. In addition to
the goals of the team or with your peers, the goal of every people leader
should be to help the direct team members be their best and make
sure they have what they need to be successful. If each team member is
more successful, the team will be more successful. The goal is not to get
the most out of each person. The paradox is that if you help direct team

members to be their best and support them with sufficient resources, they will likely expand their capabilities and exceed their production as compared to if you had only tried to "get the most out of them." In other words, if you push direct team members hard to get the most out of them without helping them to be their best, you'll only get a partial effort.

Many people leaders are intimidated by the prospect of helping direct team members be their best. Ironically, it may be easier than you think. And you likely don't have to have the answers. Instead, you need to ask the right questions.

As we look at the Enluma Leadership Model for people leaders, we'll translate how to help direct reports be their best into questions that are intended to help you take action. Building on the themes from the Foundational Leadership layer, we'll now fill in the themes of the People Leadership layer.

Team First: Create a "We before Me" culture

Specific to Team First, people leaders need to consider a few elements to be effective.

- Direct team members possess different strengths and opportunities, but together, they can be more effective.

- Finding the balance between supporting the direct team, working in the trenches, or getting out of the way.

- Use of *I* vs. *we* - These two simple words can have a very dramatic impact. The risk of a leader using *I* too much will show that it's all about you and not about the team. Think about it. A leader saying, "I want," "I said," or (Chris's personal favorite) "I'm not happy" versus, "We want," "We said," or "We're not happy," creates a very different feeling. Granted if the people leader only spoke using *we* that would be awkward and confusing. The key word here is *balance* with a priority on *we*, which is more inclusive and supportive and best reflects the "We before Me" mentality.

- Leaders should avoid saying, "My direct team" or "My team." The reason? Even if you own the business, you still don't own the people. They are not yours. Even as the people leader, you are still part of the team. Instead, by looking at the team or organization as "our team" or "our organization," conveys that everyone has equal importance.

With these insights, the People layer theme for Team First is:

People Theme for Team First: *Focus on Team's Success*

The following questions can help to *Focus on Team's Success*:

- Do you regularly share what success looks like when the direct team works well together?

- Do you regularly encourage direct team members to work through issues together?

- Do you know what the team needs to be successful?

How do you empower direct team members to work well together? These questions illustrate a tone of leading by example, "Focus on Team's Success." If your words and actions consistently show that the team (and the collective success) is more important than you (and your individual success), that is motivating and energizing for the team. Yes, you are the boss, but you don't have to remind them. They know.

Accelerate: Empower through Communication and Insights

As a people leader, there are some insights to consider for the direct team:

- Each direct team member will have perspectives and information that you do not have.

- Different people are more effective in communicating in different types of forums (1:1s, small meetings, cross functional meetings) and this preference may change based on the participants or controversiality of the topic.

- The direct team will look to you on the approach for communication, for how they should work together, and to ensure psychological safety exists.

- The direct team will watch what you do. As a people leader, direct teams will see who you give opportunities to, who you eat lunch with, and who you talk to the most.

With these insights, the People layer theme for Accelerate:

People Theme for Accelerate: *Foster Intentional Information Flow*

The following questions can help to *Foster Intentional Information Flow*:

- Do you have clear expectations for each direct team member on what their success looks like?

- With issues or challenges, do you regularly encourage the direct team to learn from mistakes and setbacks to drive improvements?

- Do you regularly have staff meetings, and do they meet the team's expectations? (Note: If you are fortunate to have direct team members reporting to you and you're not having staff meetings, seriously consider starting.)

Collectively, you can see the goal is to set a tone and create a structure enabling the ready flow of information. You don't want to create or be a roadblock to prevent the exchange of that precious commodity, information. Look for ways to ensure all teams have the information they need.

Elevate: Grow and Develop Together

Consider the dynamics of direct teams with their manager, some points to consider:

- People are happier when they are growing and learning. As mentioned earlier, this is particularly the case for Millennials and Gen Zers.

- Often, we don't spend time talking about growth interests, next potential roles, or learning opportunities.

- If you invest time and energy in developing direct team members, 19 times out of 20 they will then work harder for you and be more engaged. Why? Because they will not want to let you down. In addition, removing roadblocks along with supporting and appreciating the team can be an impactful combination

From these points, the People layer theme for Elevate is:

People Theme for Elevate: *Know and Grow the Team*

The following questions can help to *Know and Grow the Team*:

- What are the interests and career aspirations for each direct team member? (Consider short-term and long-term.)

- Have you documented the skills and capabilities the team needs to further the meaningful goals or the vision?

- How often do you talk with direct team members about their interests, and what are you doing to help them? (Note:

Mediocre to poor people leaders only talk about what direct team members can do for the leader.)

These questions address a core aspect: do you genuinely care about direct team members and want to see them do well? This is where your actions can inspire direct team members. For example, have you ever worked for a boss who didn't care?

Enluma Experience: Chris

I remember one less-than-stellar boss who, if we both received a request for our team to do work, would consistently forward me the request within minutes and ask me to do it. He was such an efficient delegator that he didn't need to leave his office (sarcasm implied). This was also very efficient in showing I was just a resource to get work done. He never asked if I was busy or if I had other priorities. He didn't care.

On the opposite end of the spectrum, one of my favorite bosses regularly asked me what I thought and asked for my input about his work. He also often checked in on me to see how I was doing to see if I was okay. On a regular basis we'd talk about my career interests, and he'd share insights and suggestions. I knew he was my boss, but he respected me, and it motivated me to not let him down. It was simple and powerful.

Which situation applies to you? Which scenario sounds more energizing?

Realize: Achieve a Powerful Destination

Often, the primary goal in an organization is simply to "get things done" or achieve results. Yes, we all have targets to achieve and expectations to meet, but focusing only on results as a people leader presents a few challenges.

- Depending upon the area or topic, you'll have to let go of control.

- Goals that have more meaning to people will be more inspiring.

- At times, you'll need to see yourself as a resource who can get things done, not just the people leader.

The risk with focusing only on results is to micromanage the team to ensure progress. If the direct team knows and appreciates the future direction of the team, they will be energized. Considering these points, the People Leadership theme for Realize is:

People Theme for Realize: *Be THE Catalyst*

The following questions can help to *Be THE Catalyst* for the direct team:

- Does each direct team member understand the "why" behind impactful goals?

- Do you know what actions and ideas direct team members have to make progress on in order to realize meaningful goals?

- What mechanisms do you have to discuss and track the progress of goals?

For the team you are given the opportunity to lead, how can you "Be THE Catalyst" to enhance progress. This can be by (1) empowering and enabling direct team members to be in the driver's seat, (2) clarifying the meaning goal, and/or (3) seeing yourself as a resource to make progress (setting the tone). If the organization is still developing the powerful destination, the direct team will likely already have meaningful goals to keep the business moving forward and improving. Until the powerful destination of the organization is clear, the direct team can focus on making progress on the existing goals.

Bringing the two initial layers together, Foundational Leadership and People Leadership, there are fundamental goals:

- Foundational Leadership - Create an environment where everyone can succeed.

- People Leadership - Empower the team to be their best.

As mentioned above in Chris's example, the most impactful leaders treat direct team members like peers and not subordinates. Whether you're the owner of a small bakery or the CEO of a Fortune 500 company, people know that you are the boss. If they see you treating them like peers, this approach will elevate their expectation of themselves. The boss wants my opinion and expects me to be part of the solution moving forward. This illustrates one of the many ways Foundational Leadership and People Leadership integrate and complement each other.

Some people may say, "This sounds exhausting. I have to help direct team members be their best while treating them like peers. Then I have to look to help my peers and myself be successful. It's too much." Instead, we recommend you take a simpler view.

Coming from a place of curiosity and caring for others, ask yourself the following:

- To be productive and work toward the meaningful goal(s), am I helping others (direct team members, peers, or stakeholders) to be successful?

- Am I only focused on my own success over others?

You may help peers and direct team members but in different ways. The fundamental goal is still the same for peers, direct team members, and an organization: sustained long-term success.

Stepping back, we encourage you to go back to the questions at the start of this chapter and utilize the themes we have outlined. Let's look at the four additional elements of the Enluma Leadership Model we added in this chapter:

	Team First Create a "We Before Me" Culture	Accelerate Empower Through Communication and Insights	Elevate Grow and Develop Together	Realize Achieve a Powerful Destination
Organizational Leadership				
People Leadership	Focus on Team's Success	Foster Intentional Information Flow	Know and Grow the Team	Be THE Catalyst
Foundational Leadership	Prioritize Shared Success	Communicate to Enable	Win Together	Build Momentum

The Glue = Trust + Fun/Enjoyment

SUMMARY

We've now filled in 8 of the 12 boxes. To enable the Enluma Leadership Model with People Leadership, we see the following themes:

Team First: Focus on Team's Success

Accelerate: Foster Intentional Information Flow

Elevate: Know and Grow the Team

Realize: Be THE Catalyst

Looking at the questions in this chapter and in Chapter 7, these questions are intended to trigger a small mindset shift.

We're not asking you to learn a new language or train for a marathon. Instead, these questions are meant to prompt a slight mindset shift to have a profound impact. If you look to help those around you and come from a place of curiosity and caring, the results can be powerful. Much like Chris's experience working with Barbara, you'll likely never forget the impact you can have.

CHAPTER 9

Organizational Leadership

> *"Life and leadership can't be about me. They have to be about us."*
>
> —Colin Powell

Two Key Priorities for Organizational Leaders

Enluma Experience: Chris

In October of 2018, I started a new role as the Global Director for Quality Control (QC) at a Fortune 100 company. The responsibilities included leading a central QC lab of a little over 100 people plus dotted-line responsibility for their thirteen manufacturing sites. If you're not familiar with QC in a company, the analysts test incoming materials used for manufacturing, intermediates, in-process materials, and finished products to ensure they meet the specifications. As you can imagine, if a material fails testing, then manufacturing and potential supply to customers could be disrupted. Being an analyst in QC is far from a low-stress job.

Analysts target to be perfect, and their work follows strict processes and procedures.

Coming into the role, I had two personal aspirations: understand and improve the culture in the central QC lab and define a strategy for all of the labs that we could align on and work together to enact. For the central lab, I had one director reporting to me, and for global QC, there was a small team working on a variety of global improvements. The biannual culture scores from the central lab were solid, but every group had opportunities. When I started with the group, I had 1:1s with the managers and director, and things sounded like they were going pretty well. We had improvement plans in place for the culture scores, our error rate for team members was very low (considering the high volume of tests that were completed each year), and there were social activities planned throughout the year to help improve the culture. I've found that if you want to understand the culture, you need to talk to as many people as possible.

Similar to the listening campaign in the call centers, to better understand what was going on, over the next few months I did 30-minute 1:1s with everyone in the organization. For each discussion, I asked the same three questions: (1) What do we do well? (2) What don't we do well? and (3) What is one thing you would do immediately if you had my job? In meetings with analysts and supervisors, I quickly learned we were out of sync. A specific 1:1 was the most memorable, with one of the strongest and most-tenured analysts. To preserve the anonymity of the discussion, we'll call him Frank. Before the 1:1, I had heard a lot of positive feedback on Frank. He consistently ran three or four complicated analyses at the same time without issue. This equated to hundreds of tests completed a year. Yes, it was impressive. Newer analysts looked up to him due to his knowledge plus his overall positive attitude. I looked forward to meeting with Frank.

In our 1:1, from the beginning I could tell Frank was nervous. He was visibly shaking and provided short answers to the questions.

> *In the middle of our 1:1, I stopped the discussion and said, "Frank, are you okay?" He replied that last year he had made two documented mistakes in the hundreds of tests he ran. I immediately realized he was worried I was going to focus on his two errors in the previous year. I quickly assured him he was a very strong analyst, and we were not going to focus on the past mistakes. After that discussion, I noticed Frank started to become calmer around me.*

Let's take another look at Frank's anxiety around his two mistakes in a year. If I'm coming from a place of curiosity, then I ask, "Why did Frank make the mistakes?" Was it because he was doing too many tests simultaneously due to our high expectations? Were the two methods related to the mistakes too complicated and temperamental (not setting analysts up for success)? If Frank is concerned about being reprimanded, then do we think he'll answer questions honestly about making the mistakes? With these questions, the analyst could perceive the conversation one of two ways:

1. How can you be perfect and not make any mistakes?

2. How do you learn from mistakes to prevent them from happening again?

Question #1 comes from a punitive position, whereas the second question comes from a place of curiosity and collaboration. Why do we share this in relation to organizational leaders? It illustrates the first of two key goals for an organizational leader:

Goal 1: Establish and foster a positive and open culture where people can thrive and excel. Illustrating this objective and another element of the 1:1s with the central lab, I repeatedly heard "I've never had a 1:1 with a director before," or "Thank you for listening." It was an initial step to show them I cared and wanted to help the team. But what was key? Sharing the progress with the entire lab of what I was hearing and what actions we were planning on taking or better yet completed. When the actions were being implemented from their feedback, that's when I started to build credibility with the entire organization. The goal was to enable open and honest feedback without the risk of any repercussions. People will gain trust and thrive in a safe culture.

Earlier in the book, we also discussed how the positive and productive workgroups occurred inconsistently. To have not just a high-performing team, but rather a high-performing organization, the organizational leader must establish a culture where people can speak up, learn, grow, and challenge each other, including the organizational leader.

You will also need to be curious about what the broader organization, not just the direct team, needs to be successful. Here is the challenge: the needs of any organization will change and evolve over time. This means that you cannot consider a one-time curiosity; ongoing curiosity for an organizational leader is critical.

The second goal for an organizational leader is tied to my second objective with the global QC labs.

Goal 2: Determine and communicate where the organization is going. When people show up to work each day, they want to feel part of something that's moving forward—an organization striving toward a better future. In short, they want to be part of a thriving organization.

To make that happen, ideas will naturally emerge from all levels of the organization. But without a clear vision of where the organization is headed, even the most well-intentioned efforts can pull in different directions—sometimes even working against the bigger picture.

On the other hand, when team members clearly understand and believe in the organization's future direction, their ideas and efforts become aligned. They begin contributing in ways that move the whole organization closer to its goals.

That's why it's essential for leadership teams not only to define a compelling future but to communicate it clearly and consistently. When that clarity exists, it energizes people—and the results can be transformational.

Enluma Experience: Chris

At the time I took the role to lead the global QC operations, we had 13 manufacturing sites spread across multiple countries in North America, Europe, and Asia. Each manufacturing site had a QC lab, and there were additional labs spread out across the network (including South America and Africa). Of the 13-plus labs, each one had their own focus and different types of products or steps within the manufacturing process (intermediate, finished goods, or packaging). Given the geographic or product differences, it quickly became apparent that we had 13 labs with different strategies and approaches. We were not aligned and had scattered pockets of people working together. Working with a sub team of leaders from the manufacturing sites, we determined that we needed a cohesive vision. To do this, we needed input from as many people as possible, so we went to work.

The sub team put together a short survey to understand our challenges and opportunities. We then tailored the survey for analysts, supervisors, and managers. Not surprisingly, we had a few language barriers but found ways to get insights. Over the course of a month, we collected data from all of the labs. Then we brought the sub team physically together in one location. We first identified the key areas where we wanted to focus (process, people, analytics, and IT systems). From there we were able to build a maturity model for each element of the process so that we can illustrate where along the maturity model we were for each of the elements. To be clear, the resulting strategy in the maturity model (endpoint) was absolutely aspirational. A cool aspect of this approach was that the aspirational end state was based on the team's input (all levels) combined with future directions noted from our senior leadership. As a quick aside, given we were working with the "analytical" labs, the use of a maturity model to measure and map our strategy proved very well received. I thought it was hilarious that we even quantified and measured our strategy.

So, what happened?

In our meetings within the subteam, we were able to identify where each lab was along the maturity model. Then with leadership, if they asked us where we wanted to go, we had a tool we could utilize. This gave our analysts a sense of where we were going. We even used the maturity model with IT colleagues to discuss our projects and where we were. It became a powerful single slide to align our teams (in every direction). We also saw how multiple projects and initiatives fit together for the aspirational end state.

Noting the two priorities for Organizational Leadership, we have questions to help you. Even if you don't have the opportunity to lead an organization, these questions will help to frame the perspective of how the organization could operate.

1. Establish and foster a positive and open culture where people can thrive and excel.

2. Determine and communicate where the organization is going.

Current State. Assess the culture and overall performance of the organization.

- In detail how would you describe the culture of the organization you have the opportunity to lead? (How did the team respond to a recent big change or project launch?)

- Do all issues come to you?

- If you were to survey the organization, do they know the future strategy of the organization?

Ideal Future State. Identify and describe the future you're striving for.

- Do you know where the organization should be in three years? This can be related to how it operates, systems that are in place, additional tools and capabilities, and the development of the people. If you don't provide a future vision, others will be more than happy to tell you what to do.

- How would you like the organization to implement solutions and address issues going forward?

- Why would someone want to work in the organization you have the opportunity to lead?

Very likely, exploring these questions can be transformational for the organization. You will identify challenges to overcome. You can see what could be or what is possible.

This may seem like common sense, but organizations and teams get busy with their day to day and don't take the time to map out the future. Additionally, many leaders (at all layers) commonly feel uncomfortable mapping out the future because we take time away from achieving results and getting things done. Here is the risk: if you don't identify the future destination with the organization, you involuntarily introduce uncertainty into the organization, and people will come up with their own ideas of where the organization is going. With uncertainty, you're likely to add unnecessary stress as people will want to know if they are going to still have a job. Without a plan, unfortunately people commonly go to a negative future vision (likely correlated to the stress from uncertainty). They will also conclude leadership is clueless and doesn't care about them. Part of this is human nature. When most people don't hear about what another group is doing (in this case the leadership team), they typically think the other group is slacking off or doing something negative.

Let's return to the two key goals of organizational leadership:

1. Establish and foster a positive and open culture where people can thrive and excel.

2. Determine and communicate where the organization is going.

You may also ask, "Do I only focus on these two goals? What about running a business?" You're right to ask. The goals are integrated into everything you do, and you need to run the business to ensure things are moving forward and work is completed. Absolutely. Alternatively, you can look at it this way:

- If the organization knows where they are going, then each employee can actively help to progress the organization and the company. It's in their best interest. Projects and initiatives are more likely to be aligned with the future direction.

- If you have a culture where employees speak up and learn from mistakes, then ideas will be better, and solutions will be implemented faster. Issues or problems will also be addressed more quickly.

Another wrinkle to all of this? Even more so than for a people leader, the broader organization is watching you very closely and will follow your lead. If you are always focused on the day to day, fighting fires, and always in the details, then what tone do you think you're setting for the organization? Firefighting is rewarded and encouraged. Conversely, if you are only ever talking about the future and what could be, then the team will likely think you don't care about today or what they do. So, balance is key.

Up to this point, we have two out of three rows filled in with the themes to utilize the Enluma Leadership Model. This now takes us to how we can utilize the model related to these key goals.

Team First: Create a "We before Me" culture

Specific to the attitude of Team First, organizational leaders need to consider a few elements to be effective.

- **Resist mediocrity.** There is a reason we needed a leadership insight focused on humility in both the people and organizational leadership chapters. Organizational leaders are more likely to think "me before we"—the exact opposite of the "Team First" goal. Here is the bigger risk: if you think you are the most important team member, then people will focus less on the best ideas or solutions and more on what looks best to you. People are less likely to be engaged in their work because they will think their idea doesn't matter. It becomes a game of who can impress the organizational leader. Unknowingly if you take this approach, you risk encouraging mediocrity in a race to make you happy.

- **Use restraint to enable the team.** Losing humility also makes it increasingly more difficult to utilize restraint. If you believe your ideas are the best and you're the most important, then why don't people just follow you? Restraint becomes critical for an organizational leader, so team members can speak up and are not bombarded by additional work and requests from "the big boss" that may seem important to you but run the risk of derailing the team.

- **Unlock ideas from the organization.** With thinking about being a part of the organization, there is a significant opportunity. You'll see that good ideas and solutions can come from all parts of the organization because people will see (even if it's with time), that their ideas matter and more importantly, they are part of the solution or changes. This is huge for the energy and engagement of the organization. While it sounds difficult, the key piece is the organization knowing ideas and solutions that are implemented come from everywhere in the organization.

With these points, the Organizational layer theme for Team First is:

Organizational Theme for Team First: *Energize the Organization*

Moving forward, the following questions can help to *Energize the Organization*:

- Do we regularly solve issues or challenges by engaging experts and others throughout the organization?

- Does the leadership team encourage a structure of healthy debate and consider different viewpoints?

- Does the organization have the tools and capabilities to provide ideas and feedback to leadership?

How can you translate humility of the organizational leader to a strong culture? Focus on the best solution regardless of where it comes from, or in other words, the winning solution. Institute the goal of the Energize the Organization. Focusing on solutions and moving forward along with an approach where everyone can provide good ideas can be powerful. Solutions should be thought of as applied ideas that are time bound. Anyone can sit and brainstorm on what could happen and how things should work, but taking those ideas and looking for the practical application to move forward or address problems can be powerful. The solutions cannot be dependent upon the title or role of the originator. People will also feel empowered if they know the organizational leader is looking for and requesting input from them. When solutions are developed and implemented, people feel safe knowing their thoughts are valued and they are part of the solution.

With team-first values, the information commodity is considered more important than ego and title.

Accelerate: Empower through Communication and Insights

As an organizational leader, there are some points you need to consider:

- You are now even further removed from the day and will not have all of the information. Your exposure to data is likely limited to key issues or deliverables, but the organization has the data and information.

- The organization will be looking to you to set the tone with supervisors/managers (people leaders). Also, within this, the organization will follow your lead in setting the tone in response to opportunities and challenges.

- Regular updates from the organizational leader (even if just emails), will be appreciated by the majority of the team. We challenge you to get creative in how you communicate. Assuming you're not sending a note about how awesome or important you are (hint: don't do that).

With these points, the Organizational layer theme for Accelerate is:

Organizational Theme for Accelerate: *Illuminate the Path*

The following questions can help to *Illuminate the Path*:

- How can you improve alignment for the broader organization on the "why" behind key goals and plans shared by the leadership team?

- Does the leadership team regularly encourage and seek feedback from the broader organization?

- Does the leadership team provide periodic updates to reinforce the future destination along with progress or upcoming changes?

Have you ever tried to walk on a path in the woods or a forest at night? Even with a flashlight it can be tricky. You can only see where your flashlight shines, and the overall darkness seems disorienting with the shadows and limited ability to gauge depth, and what is near and far. If you're just going for a hike without a destination, you may want to wait until it's light out. On the other hand, if you know where you're going, but the path is not lit, the journey will be nerve-wracking.

Now take our walk example and compare it to the business world. If you are given a future strategy (where the organization is going) by your leadership without an invitation to participate or without short- and longer-term needs or objectives, it's like trying to take a hike in the dark—difficult to know where to take steps and easy to lose the direction toward the destination.

Herein lies the opportunity for organizational leadership. Utilize communication and information to *illuminate the path* for the organization. As we'll talk more in the Realize portion of the Enluma Leadership Model (clear destination), the goal with communication from an organizational leader is to illuminate the path for the organization. If people know the direction of the organization and the path is illuminated, they will be more likely to take the path and move forward. Additionally, if the path is illuminated, you're encouraging the organization to come forward. Yes, there will be some uncertainty far off in the darkness and shadows, and there likely will be multiple paths, which will require leadership and team decision making. However, if the path is lit and people know where they are going, the organization will be more successful.

Elevate: Grow and Develop Together

Below are some insights we observed with our experiences and survey responses:

- People can be intimidated by more senior leaders in an organization. As a result, there are opportunities to show you care about the broader organization by spending time with them and learning about what they do. Even if you did the job previously, things have likely changed or improved, and team members need to see you as a real person.

- What will motivate the organization is knowing the organizational leader cares about the organization, as shown by sharing the leader's time.

- Inspirational leaders take actions that show recognition and appreciation, and create fun for the team.

- Inspirational leaders prioritize team and individual development instead of personal (upward) success. Most team members want to be challenged and grow their careers; investing in team and personal development is a critical objective of any organization.

From these insights, the Organizational layer theme for Elevate is:

Organizational Theme for Elevate: *Be an Authentic Part of the Team*

Moving forward, the following questions can help to *Be an Authentic Part of the Team*:

- What are the organization's strengths, challenges, and opportunities?

- Does the leadership team have regular opportunities to receive feedback on their performance?

- How frequently does the leadership team meet with team members to understand their roles and the daily challenges they encounter?

If you see yourself as the most important person on the team, then all decisions, updates, changes, issues, and challenges need to go through you. Yes, it likely will make you feel important, but as you can imagine, you risk being a bottleneck. Remember, as the organizational leader you are part of the team. As mentioned in the prior chapter, your responsibilities differ from other team members, but that doesn't mean you are not part of the team. This is the mindset shift if you truly see yourself as part of the team:

At first pass, you're likely thinking that this sounds like an idyllic love fest where everything is great. Quite the contrary. If you support the team during challenging times by removing roadblocks, showing support, or being in the trenches with them, they will appreciate it. As you work with the team to define the strategy, you'll also have insights into potential hurdles for the strategy. Your time is precious, but it's critical that you understand the challenges and obstacles the team faces.

If you propose unrealistic approaches or goals because you don't understand the regular challenges of the team, you will lose credibility. You'd be seen as out of touch with the organization, and you will sacrifice results.

Realize: Achieve a Powerful Destination

We all love results. Following are key insights that combine organizational leadership and results:

- The importance of leaders focusing on team strategy and where the organization is going to align teams and show you care

- The ability to gauge projects and improvements against the future state goal (especially if people are empowered to come up with solutions)

- Instituting ways to make challenges and opportunities visible to create transparency and activate the organization to solicit and prioritize thoughts and ideas

- Empowering the organization to address key issues or challenges, taking a weight off of your shoulders.

- Believing that good ideas come from everywhere, and unleashing the team

Integrating these points, we can define the Organizational layer theme for Realize.

Organizational Theme for Realize: *Outline the Destination and the Path*

Moving forward, the following questions can help to *Outline the Destination and the Path*:

- Do you have a clear understanding of the organization's desired future direction?

- Are the cultural expectations for how the organization should operate to achieve the future destination clear?

- What is the communication plan to provide transparency on the future state strategy?

Likely the most "well duh" statement in the book, the organizational leader is responsible for ensuring the destination is meaningful and achievable. The destination should also be aspirational and noble. It should be a stretch. To increase the success, there should be elements the organization provided input into (similar to the approach Chris took with the QC labs). With this approach, people will have a seat on the "change bus" as opposed to being hit by it.

We know people typically don't like change, so, the communication plan, including team members input is key. Then they see what is in it for them toward a better future. In effect the strategy plus the communication plan will "Outline the Destination and the Path."

Stepping back, we encourage you to reflect on the four Organizational Leadership elements of the Enluma Leadership Model we added in this chapter:

	Team First Create a "We Before Me" Culture	Accelerate Empower Through Communication and Insights	Elevate Grow and Develop Together	Realize Achieve a Powerful Destination
Organizational Leadership	Energize the Organization	Illuminate the Path	Be an Authentic Part of the Team	Outline the Destination & the Path
People Leadership	Focus on Team's Success	Foster Intentional Information Flow	Know and Grow the Team	Be THE Catalyst
Foundational Leadership	Prioritize Shared Success	Communicate to Enable	Win Together	Build Momentum

The Glue = Trust + Fun/Enjoyment

SUMMARY

Collectively for organizational leaders it all ties back to key objectives:

1. Establish and foster a positive and open culture where people can thrive and excel.

2. Determine and communicate where the organization is going.

Now let's add the two goals for the two initial layers (remember additive layers):

- Foundational Leadership - Create an environment where everyone can succeed.

- People Leadership - Empower the team to be at their best.

We have now filled in all 12 boxes. To enable the Enluma Leadership Model with Organizational Leadership, we see:

- **Team First:** Energize the Organization

- **Accelerate:** Illuminate the Path

- **Elevate:** Be an Authentic Part of the Team

- **Realize:** Outline the Destination and the Path

Connecting the three layers together, organizational leaders have direct team members reporting into them and have peers. The Enluma Leadership Model is not as effective for an organizational leader if you only focus on the organizational layer. Organizational Leadership is the most powerful when you work on all three layers. For example, if an organizational leader only focuses on the strategy and culture of the team (key goals of organizational leadership) but does not focus on developing direct teams or working really well with peers, what happens? Direct teams may become disengaged, and the organization runs the risk of being separated from other organizations because the leaders are not speaking. The organization will be limited. Conversely, what happens if the organizational leader focuses on peers and developing direct team members but not building the strategy and defining the culture? The broader organization will see the leader as out of touch, and progress will be limited. The full power and impact reside with all three layers together, not separate.

PART 4

Your Journey

CHAPTER 10

The Destination and the Plan

"The way to get started is to quit talking and begin doing."

—Walt Disney

Enluma Experience: Chris

In 2017, I took part in a broader development program. One area of focus within the program was presentation skills. Similar to most presentation skills classes, we completed short presentations with a partner and noted the filler words like, um, or so, paid attention to posture and hand movements, and noted how we engaged the room (eye contact and body language). After we practiced in pairs, we were asked to present on an unknown occupation assigned to us when we got to the front of the room. Talk about thinking on your feet! I was assigned to present my new career, Sears Tower window washer. As we improvised our fictitious career (many achieving humorous results, including one participant who got a professional curler [as in the sport curling] and thought it was a professional hair curler). Viewers then

> *pointed out strengths and areas of opportunity. Each person took turns until everyone received feedback and actions to practice.*
>
> *Everyone in the class then formulated a plan on what to improve in their next presentation. They looked for opportunities to get better and apply what we had just learned.*

After years of reading leadership books illustrating the value and impact of leadership or autobiographies that talked about experiences of leaders, we often don't look for opportunities to practice or improve our leadership. When taking any leadership class, you may remember one or two points that you practice for a few months and then risk forgetting them. Why can't leadership training be more like presentation skills where you build an action plan and have clear skills to practice?

Similar to presentation skills, the Enluma Leadership Model can be utilized in meetings, 1:1s, client conversations, with planning growth and career development (for yourself or others). The model can also be integrated into annual performance reviews, hiring practices, and countless other areas. If you truly want to develop yourself or others as inspirational leaders, applying the model will enable many transformations.

Key Factors in Your Journey

With application of the model, there are three key factors to be considered:

1. Being honest with ourselves

2. The paradox of habits

3. Application, Application, Application

We'll review these three factors and then talk about defining your destination along with how to map your journey.

Being honest with ourselves. There are two aspects where we need to be honest with ourselves. We've worked to make this book concise and to have a logical and intuitive model to develop inspirational leaders. Our goal was to utilize data, stories, and literature to make our case for the value of and dire need for more inspirational leaders. On the basis of this, we want to help you to apply the Enluma Leadership Model using the power of questions to reinforce the various themes. Here is our first aspect where we need to be honest.

By reading this book, you are not guaranteed to be an inspirational leader. There is no "one-and-done" approach to inspirational leadership. As you will have hopefully concluded, it takes investing time, hard work, strong motivation and allowing yourself to be vulnerable to achieve the desired inspirational outcomes.

For better or for worse, you will need to define and then map out your journey, which is not likely to be an overnight transformation. Going through the book, you probably noticed where you are stronger in some areas of the Enluma Leadership Model and where you have opportunities to improve. If that is the case, you've already started your journey.

With any journey, you need to define a destination. Herein lies the second aspect of honesty: you define your destination. This is why we have utilized questions throughout the book around the impact you want to have. You have the answers. You define the type of inspirational leader you want to be and the impact you want to have. With your destination, there are a few additional points to consider:

First: The destination is not a specific position (Manager, Owner, Vice President, etc.). Instead, the destination is how *you* want to operate, regardless of your role.

Second: Your unique destination is not better or worse than someone else's. Some people may enjoy working without direct reports and aspire to be an exceptionally strong individual contributor who demonstrates exceptional Foundational Leadership, while another person may want to be a great C-suite leader who excels in all three layers of leadership. It is important to acknowledge and respect this.

Third: *You* define the timeline and the pace. Can you work to improve in all three layers at once in a year? Some people might. Others may want to be intentional and focus on one layer at a time as habits take time and focus to change (more on that later).

Fourth: There is power in working with peers and/or a coach—the partner approach. We know that if we partner with others, there will be a self-imposed pressure to make progress (even if your partner is not providing any pressure). The partner approach also ties back to the motivation of not letting the other person down. If you see the value of becoming an inspirational leader, we strongly encourage you to take others on your journey. It's also more fun.

The paradox of habits. The basal ganglia region of the brain controls habits[38]. We make choices (good or bad) on a regular basis without much thought. Habits develop unconsciously, such as the hand you use to brush your teeth, the motion you use to put on your seatbelt, or how you use utensils to eat. For most of these activities, it's good that we don't have to actively control them. It would take a lot more energy. What is the paradox of habits? The first time you do something requires intentional control or management via the prefrontal cortex. With repetition, control of the activity gradually transfers from your prefrontal cortex to your basal ganglia, so you no longer have to intentionally control the activities. Think about going to a new grocery store. The first few times you consciously note where you are going to locate items. A few months later you can find items in that store without thinking about it. The activity has shifted from the frontal cortex to the basal ganglia.

You may have read that habits take 10,000 hours of practice or repetition for them to form (and shift to the basal ganglia). That, or it's the number of hours practicing an instrument before you're good enough to play in Carnegie Hall. With habit formation, there is a lot of debate on the number of repetitions or hours, and it likely depends upon the person or the activity. Where we see commonality is that there are ways to help yourself be more successful[39,40] with building new habits, such as improving your inspirational leadership skills.

- **Clarify the "why."** With this book, we've illustrated the value of inspirational leadership and the characteristics. If your goal is to be a strong inspirational leader, then it will be key to remind yourself of your destination to maintain momentum. Why do you personally want to be an inspirational leader, and what is the impact you want to have on yourself and others? Answers to these two questions can be your "why."

- **Combine with a daily task.** Integrate the new behaviors into existing activities (more on that later with building your journey). With this approach you're not adding a new task but instead modifying an existing meeting or task.

- **Remember that perfection is the enemy of success.** As people build new habits, there will be weeks or even months where it doesn't go well. People make mistakes, and this is an opportunity to practice self-compassion. If you slip up, that's okay. What is important is to make adjustments and continue forward even if you stumble. Remember roughly right is better than precisely wrong.

- **Measure your progress.** A weekly or monthly review can help to track your progress. As part of the measurement, it's good to also reflect on how you're doing and whether you need to take a different approach.

- **Give yourself time.** Part of the challenge is we think we will change our behaviors overnight. You'll know you've formed a new habit when the behavior starts to occur more naturally.

We share the above insights on habits with you for a few reasons. First, forming habits requires intentionality and persistence, but knowing the above "habit accelerators" can help you be more successful. We will integrate the above insights into helping you build your journey (more on that later).

Application, Application, Application. Reading the earlier chapters, you may have wondered why we had questions asking about how you lead today compared to where you'd like to be. We also use questions to activate each theme of the Enluma Leadership Model. The questions can prompt you to envision how you'd like to lead and to spark the initial view of your destination.

Integrating questions into existing activities or meetings can be an easier way to progress along your journey. Questions from a place of curiosity can challenge you and others around you in a productive and positive way. In the next chapters, we'll start mapping out your journey.

Deciding your Focus

Now we get to the key application of the model, clarifying the focus of your journey. There is no wrong choice of where you'd like to focus, and your answer will likely evolve as you grow and change. The good news? You have three options to choose from:

1. Foundational Leadership

2. Foundational and People Leadership

3. Foundational, People, and Organizational Leadership

After reading the previous chapters these options are probably not a surprise. We recommend everyone start with Foundational Leadership, as it is the base for the other two leadership layers. We also know that some people may need to work on multiple layers at the same time, which can be more challenging. Remember, to grow and develop, leverage your organizational development planning process, and develop a SMART development plan.

Some people may say they want to choose Option #3 because it's the most glamorous and likely to have the largest paycheck. But here is where you really need to assess where you are today and what you need to improve first to better prepare yourself for the future. The goal is to enable your long-term success, not achieve glamor.

Mapping Your Journey

Now that you have an initial destination for your journey. We'll start mapping the path. This is where you identify the themes from the Enluma Leadership Model that represent the most opportunity for you in your role today and to support future aspirations. How can you identify the themes that you need to prioritize? You'll be the most uncomfortable with the questions because you won't have or won't like your answer. Your path will focus first on where you need to improve. As you progress, you will likely shift your path and work to other themes to reinforce or challenge yourself, thereby (re)shaping the path of your journey. You may also decide to dig further into the same theme by adding more questions. That is also a good approach.

To define the themes presenting the most opportunity, there are three recommended approaches for each of the leadership layers to be the most impactful.

Foundational Leadership Layer - Self-assessment

- Review the statements and score your comfort level with each.

- Based on your individual review, you'll see the themes and questions where you can improve (scored the lowest).

- Optionally, you can ask a peer for feedback to provide a more reflective approach on all or some of the questions.

People Leadership Layer - Parallel approach (with direct team)

- We recommend a parallel path, where you identify your weakest themes by scoring the statements.

- At the same time, the direct team scores the statements and records the average score per statement, with the intention of providing you feedback.

- Then with a combined review, you'll see where your answers are different (potential blindspots), giving you better insights to map out your journey.

Organizational Leadership Layer - Phased approach (direct team then broader organization)

- For the organizational layer, we recommend a multi-step approach. Start by working with the direct leadership team and then further improve the initial plan with input and feedback from the broader organization.

- This approach both illustrates (1) the higher degree of complexity to be a strong organizational leader and (2) the opportunity to develop the direct team as organizational leaders in the process.

In the subsequent chapters we'll leverage the different Enluma Leadership Model layers to define your destination and how to map your journey. Our starting point is the Foundational Leadership Layer.

SUMMARY

As you begin developing your plan to grow as an inspirational leader, this chapter covered:

1. Honest Self-Assessments: Creating a personal development plan that is both ambitious and realistic.

2. Habit Formation Science: Using proven habit accelerators to strengthen new leadership behaviors.

3. Leveraging Questions for Growth: Integrating thoughtful questions into everyday interactions to drive development.

4. Building Your Roadmap: Identifying key focus areas and structuring a clear path forward.

CHAPTER 11

Enluma Leadership Model for Foundational Leadership

For the Foundational Leadership Layer, we'll review the themes and related questions for each of the four elements. For your journey map, the goal is to identify where you need to improve, and we encourage you to take a hard look at the summary for each theme. For example, with Team First, the theme is "Prioritize Shared Success" and the details were discussed in Chapter 7.

We will guide you through Foundational Leadership to define your opportunities and how to practice so the questions become habits. The pace for your journey is up to you. The Foundational Layer truly is the base of inspirational leadership. Fundamentally, the important part is building the habits and use of the questions to progress along your journey.

How to Build Your Journey

A key element of building your journey is to understand where you have the biggest opportunity to grow and develop. To enable the assessment of your opportunities, below you will find the statement equivalents to the questions from each of the chapters where we applied the Enluma to each layer. Take a look through these statements and assess your comfort level with each. Score the statements from 1 (Complete Disagreement) to 5 (Complete Agreement). After you have scored all of the statements, calculate the total score for each theme. We'll then have questions at the end of the exercise to start your journey.

Our comfort level rating scale from 1 to 5 is explained as follows:

1 - Completely Disagree: The statement causes significant discomfort or unease. Immediate changes are necessary to improve.

2 - Disagree: There is noticeable discomfort, but it is manageable.

3 - Neutral: Conditions are neither comfortable nor uncomfortable. Neutral feelings prevail, and nothing has been raised as a concern.

4 - Agree: The situation or environment feels good, with few or no issues causing discomfort.

5 - Completely Agree: Everything is ideal, and you feel strongly that you have this statement under control.

Bonus Resources

To facilitate building your journey with all three layers, we have printable worksheets available on our website (www.enlumagroup.com/book).

Team First: Prioritize Shared Success

The intention is to focus on the shared success of peers and yourself. If a peer struggles, then you struggle and vice versa. Think of a basketball team. If one player on the court is struggling, this will significantly decrease the likelihood of success for the team.

Statements to Score	Rating (1 to 5)
You understand what your peers need to maximize collaboration (work most effectively together).	
You consistently emphasize the power of collaboration to achieve greater results together.	
You regularly demonstrate that your success is closely linked to the success of your peers.	
Total Score	

For the ratings 1 = Completely Disagree to 5 = Completely Agree

Accelerate: Communicate to Enable

With this theme, the goal is to equip yourself and peers with the insights and clear expectations to be successful. The below statements are intended to challenge how you share and receive information along with clarity of expectations for each other.

Statements to Score	Rating (1 to 5)
In challenging situations, you stay calm, setting a tone of confidence and determination.	
With mistakes and issues, you regularly look to understand the root cause and identify solutions, not cast blame.	
You regularly share information and data with peers without them asking.	
Total Score	

For the ratings 1 = Completely Disagree to 5 = Completely Agree

Elevate: Win Together

In some ways this theme is an extension of Team First. With "Win Together," the idea is you are part of something bigger than each individual and a higher degree of success comes in partnership with peers.

With a wider view, you can see the challenges and opportunities facing the team, not just yourself.

Statements to Score	Rating (1 to 5)
You actively look for ways to help peers address challenges.	
You adjust your approach to engage with challenging peers to improve the situations. You think about what you can do differently.	
You often connect with peers to talk about the challenges they face.	
Total Score	

For the ratings 1 = Completely Disagree to 5 = Completely Agree

Realize: Build Momentum

Groups of people often spend time mapping out and defining a meaningful and even transformational future, but the risk is stopping with the visualization. Making progress and building momentum is critical for the (long-term) success of the group.

Statements to Score	Rating (1 to 5)
You have plans and goals to build momentum with your peers, either toward a meaningful future destination or, if no specific destination is defined, toward improving collective performance.	
You understand roadblocks to making progress (including short- and long-term) and are working to address or prevent them.	
You discuss meaningful goals with your peers in a way that enables progress and building momentum.	
Total Score	

For the ratings 1 = Completely Disagree to 5 = Completely Agree

Additional Insights

The themes and questions you scored the lowest highlight your opportunities. If you want to progress as an inspirational leader, this is where you can focus your initial efforts. Integrate efforts to improve on the themes and questions into your existing meetings and routines. This is the equivalent of practicing new presentation skills, and remember: "practice makes perfect." A suggestion: copy these questions into your (physical or digital) notebook to keep them readily available.

When issues or challenges arise, these questions will prove invaluable. When times are harder, it's easier to be negative, to miss problems, to be judgmental, and to be swept up by emotions. The goal is to be curious, remain calm, and help yourself and others be better in harder times. Then with repetition, challenges will become easier. For example, looking at the first question for Team First, "Do you understand what your peers need to maximize collaboration or work more effectively together," you can add "to address this challenge or issue" to the end of the question thus applying to a recent issue or challenge. Taking this approach will make you better. You'll inspire others to "do more and become more." Inspiring yourself and others can enable you to better manage and overcome adversity.

Action Planning

Noted in the previous chapter, we'll leverage multiple "habit hacks" to improve your probability of success.

1. **Define your why.** After reading through this book, why do you want to progress as an inspirational Foundational leader? (*Important to clarify your personal why*)

2. **Identify your opportunities.** How do you want to improve the Statements where you scored the lowest? Additionally, what existing meetings, teams, or tasks could be good opportunities to improve your comfort level?

3. **Determine your success.** What is the best way to measure your progress or how you are increasing your comfort level with the above Statements? We recommend making this simple and very manageable so tracking doesn't become a chore. For example, you could do a quick progress check every Friday morning to rescore your comfort level to see your progress.

4. **Build your support.** Who would you like to partner with (if you don't have someone already) to help you along your journey?

5. **Look deeper into your scoring.**

   a. What are the two easiest and two hardest statements for you? Why are they so different in your comfort levels? What could be triggering the differences?

   b. For the two lowest-scoring statements, what can you do in the next three to four weeks to increase your scoring toward a 4 or 5? When you think of these two statements, what does a score of 4 or 5 look like (in detail)? Once you make progress on the two lowest-scored statements, you can then shift to the next two lowest scored and continue until you've addressed all of your lowest-scored statements.

   c. Of the four themes, where did you score the highest and the lowest? How will improving on the lowest-scoring scenarios help you to improve for the lowest-scored themes?

6. **Set your goals.** Noting the scores for themes and statements, what progress would you like to make in three, six, or twelve months? In detail, how do you want to progress in the coming months? This becomes your destination of your Foundational Leadership path.

CHAPTER 12

Enluma Leadership Model for People Leadership

Enluma Experience: Jan

As part of my career, I spent a little over two years as an expatriate in Puerto Rico. During my early days on the island, I noticed that everyone showed up late to meetings, which I considered annoying and disrespectful. I had the full team sign a statement that from that moment forward, they would make an effort to show up on time. Do you think it worked? No, of course not. What I failed to realize is that in Puerto Rico, punctuality and timeliness are valued less than living life, socializing, and connecting with people. Once I grasped the reality of the cultural differences (the Dutch are known to be beyond punctual), I realized that to build genuine collaborations and relationships my approach had to change. Keeping my authenticity and incorporating cultural awareness created a more cohesive team and enabled us to achieve our desired outcomes.

I want to make it clear that this is not intended to be a perspective in cross-cultural or cross-borders management. This example reinforces the importance of understanding and inspiring the culture for shared achievement and to ensure that everyone can perform at their best.

For People Leadership, the goal is to create an environment where direct team members can be their best individually and together. With the story from Puerto Rico, we see that sometimes you have to change yourself to improve your ability to lead a direct team.

Now, we wish there was an approach that would immediately transform you and the direct team. In reality, progress requires intentionality, time, trust, and working together with the direct team. When you make progress, both you and the direct team will be glad you invested the time and energy.

How to Build Your Journey

To begin your journey to develop your People Leadership, we recommend a parallel approach.

- **Self-Assessment (People Leader).** By yourself, score the statements based on your comfort level (1 = very uncomfortable to 5 = very comfortable).

- **Team Assessment (Direct Team).** In parallel, ask the direct team to score you on the statements. They will then calculate the average score per scenario (to provide a degree of anonymity).

- **Score Review.** Decide whether to review the average team scores with the direct team (recommended) or separately. The purpose of the review is to identify opportunities and to build an action plan.

Bonus Resources

Similar to the Foundational Layer, printable worksheets are available on our website (www.enlumagroup.com/book/). This includes a sheet for the direct team to record their scores together and calculate the average.

For the following scoring, you as a people leader enter the scores received from the direct team.

Team First: Focus on Team's Success

If the direct team does well, this is a force multiplier. They will look to have larger successes with more difficult challenges and expect stronger performance. This is why it's critical to prioritize the success of the team and enable them to work strongly together.

Statements to Score	Self Rating (1 to 5)	Direct Team (1 to 5)
You regularly share what the direct team can achieve by working well together.		
You regularly encourage direct team members to work through issues together.		
You regularly ask the direct team for input and their feedback.		
Total Scores		

For the ratings 1 = Completely Disagree to 5 = Completely Agree

Accelerate: Foster Intentional Information Flow

It's key to value and share the information commodity. This includes both the data and insights in order to excel and the clarity to understand what success looks like. It is also important to understand how you, as the leader, impact the flow of information within the team.

Statements to Score	Self Rating (1 to 5)	Direct Team (1 to 5)
You have clear expectations for each direct team member on what their success looks like.		

Statements to Score	Self Rating (1 to 5)	Direct Team (1 to 5)
With issues or challenges, you regularly encourage the direct team to learn from mistakes and setbacks to drive improvements.		
Your staff meetings are held regularly and consistently meet the direct team's expectations.		
Total Scores		

For the ratings 1 = Completely Disagree to 5 = Completely Agree

Elevate: Know and Grow the Team

To help the team enable their success, you need to know each direct team member's strengths and opportunities along with their career interests. As challenges become more complex, the team needs everyone to grow and in turn increase their capabilities.

Statements to Score	Self Rating (1 to 5)	Direct Team (1 to 5)
You know the interests and career aspirations for each direct team member (both short-term and long-term).		
You encourage the direct team to develop skills and capabilities to grow and develop.		
You regularly talk with direct team members about their developmental interests.		
Total Scores		

For the ratings 1 = Completely Disagree to 5 = Completely Agree

Realize: Be THE Catalyst

The direct team is watching. If they see you focus on their success, actively remove obstacles, reward their progress, and take action, this will be a significant driver for team momentum.

Statements to Score	Self Rating (1 to 5)	Direct Team (1 to 5)
Direct team members understand the "why" behind impactful goals.		
You consistently encourage the direct team to identify and implement actions and ideas that drive progress and help achieve meaningful goals.		
You have systems in place to discuss and track the progress of goals with the direct team.		
Total Scores		

For the ratings 1 = Completely Disagree to 5 = Completely Agree

Additional Insights

With your review and the feedback of direct team members, you will then be able to prioritize where you can make progress together. This approach can also go a long way to develop increased trust with the direct team, especially when you then take actions based on their input. With the improvements, integrate the changes within your existing meetings to increase the probability of success.

Action Planning

Similar to Foundational Leadership, let's leverage the "habit accelerators."

1. **Define your why.** After reading this book, why do you want to progress as an inspirational people leader? (*Clarify your personal why. You may also choose to share this with the direct team.*)

2. **Identify your opportunities.** How do you want to improve the answers for the statements where you scored the lowest? Additionally with the direct team, what existing meetings, teams, or tasks could be good opportunities to improve your comfort level?

3. **Define your success.** What is the best way to measure your progress? Similar to Foundational Leadership, we recommend this be simple. For example, you could let the direct team know you're going to ask for their input and suggestions during 1:1s, and/or you can also gauge yourself with a short pulse check once a week.

4. **Build your support.** In addition to the direct team, is there another people leader you would like to partner with (if you don't have someone already) to help progress each other's journey?

5. **Look deeper into your scoring.**

   a. What are the two highest and two lowest statements you scored, and how did this differ with the input from the direct team? What could be triggering the differences in (1) your scores and (2) comparing your scores to the team's?

   b. For the two lowest-scoring statements, what can you do in the next three to four weeks to progress those toward a score of 4 or 5? When you think of these two statements, what does a score of 4 or 5 look like (in detail)?

   c. Of the four themes, where did you score the highest and the lowest? What is contributing to the reason for the difference in scoring?

6. **Outline your path.** Noting the scores for themes and statements, what progress would you like to make in three, six, or twelve months? In detail, how do you want to progress in the coming months? This becomes your destination of your Foundational Leadership path.

CHAPTER 13

Enluma Leadership Model for Organizational Leadership

Enluma Experience: Jan

As part of a global integration, I spent time in the United Arab Emirates (UAE), the United Kingdom (UK), and the Netherlands. The Fortune 100 company I worked for bought a smaller company and asked to integrate all operations including moving warehouses in UAE and the Netherlands to existing warehousing infrastructure in six months. At first view, this seemed an impossible task. Who could integrate all operations disciplines and a warehouse (including manufacturing set-up) in 180 days? We approached this essentially using the Enluma Leadership Model: I created the destination, the path, and the associated timeline. The path was illuminated through collaborative strategy sessions and a communication strategy to ensure progress on the journey. Team members were empowered to support the lofty goal, and what initially seemed impossible actually became possible: we found a new warehouse in Europe and moved the inventory plus manufacturing operations, the warehouse in UAE was closed, and all operations were integrated.

For people leaders, there is real power in working with direct team members to become an inspirational leader. When leading an organization, it is likely the team is larger, the environment more complex, and including the organization on the journey is more critical. Fundamentally, the role of a strong organizational leader is to align and direct the organization, starting with the leadership team. The integration story we shared above is a great example of utilizing the Enluma Leadership Model to direct the organization by mapping out the destination and expectations to achieve incredible results. A similar approach can be leveraged for any organization to deliver well beyond what you think is possible. For these approaches, we recommend a stepwise approach.

Achieving Incredible Results

Step 1: Identify the strategic destination and the culture to enable the future.

- Defining the destination and culture is the definition of a team sport. With this analogy, the organizational leader acts as the coach, the captain, and a hybrid player.

- As a coach of the leadership team, the goal is to steer and point discussions and analyses in the right direction (toward an aspirational and achievable strategy and enabling culture).

- As the captain, the organizational leader has the final decision-making rights and is the tiebreaker.

- As a player, the organizational leader partners with the direct team and broader organization to build both the future destination and the enabling culture. This approach also models the behaviors needed to partner together, challenge each other, and define a better future.

- The scores for the assessment per the Organizational Leadership layer elements will integrate input from the direct leadership team, and the overall process is steered, course-corrected, and owned by the organizational leader.

Step 2: Share the initial strategic destination and culture expectations with the organization.

- Similar to step 1, the organizational leader steers the organization and reiterates the importance of a robust and aspirational vision that will challenge and grow the organization.

- Having defined focus areas, the organizational leader asks members of the direct leadership team to own or co-own one of the focus areas of the strategic destination.

- The organizational leader stresses the importance of pressure testing the initial destination and culture with the broader organization.

Step 3: Plan for keeping the progress alive and evolving while integrating into your identity as an organization.

- The organizational leader is critical for setting the expectations of clear plans and regular status updates for each focus area of the journey.

- The organizational leader encourages celebrating and recognizing the broader team when milestones are achieved.

Note: The goal of the first step is to define a future and culture the entire organization can get behind. The organizational leader drives the effort with significant input from the direct leadership team.

How to Build Your Journey

If you already have a strong vision defined, then the organizational layer focuses on enabling the existing vision for sustained success. If you don't have a vision, we'll guide you through an easy approach to build your initial vision with the direct leadership team.

Bonus Resources

Similar to the Foundational and People Leadership layers, printable worksheets are available on our website (www.enlumagroup.com/book/).

Step 1: Identify the strategic destination and the culture to enable the future

Before starting this step, we need to revisit the two key objectives of an organizational leader:

1. Determine and communicate where the organization is going.

2. Establish and foster a positive and open culture where people can thrive and excel.

Noting these underlying goals, the organizational layer is not evenly weighted between the four elements of the model.

- Realize: Achieve a Powerful Destination is the primary element.

- Team First, Accelerate, and Elevate work to enable achieving the powerful destination.

Noting this weighting, the scoring will start with Realize, followed by a discussion about the vision and culture of the organization. If you have a pre-existing and strong vision, then the scoring of Realize may go quickly. The evaluation of the other three elements then works to reinforce and elevate the pre-existing vision and culture.

In terms of the initial scoring, this is completed as a team with the organizational leader having the final input and decision-making rights. Each leadership team member can score the questions separately or work together in a meeting, whatever works best for how the team operates. Regardless of how the initial scoring is completed, it's important to discuss and align on the final scores. This approach also encourages ownership by the leadership team. If the organizational leader solely provides the direction, then the leadership team is not an active participant on the journey toward the future. The team needs to work together knowing the organizational leader is the final decision-maker.

Note: For all of these exercises when sharing insights or thoughts, we recommend that the leader of the team speaks last for all inputs (not to steer the team). This also shows respect to the broader team.

Realize: Outline the Destination and the Journey

As mentioned above, the cornerstone of Organizational Leadership is establishing the destination and the culture to enable it. If you don't have a strategic destination defined, or it wasn't developed with broader input, inspiring an organization will be limited.

Statements to Score	Team Rating (1 to 5)
You have a clear understanding of the organization's desired future direction.	
The cultural expectations for how the organization should operate to achieve and sustain the better future are clear.	
You are confident the organization will be successful in the future.	
Total Score	

For the ratings 1 = Completely Disagree to 5 = Completely Agree

Realize Analysis

As a leadership team, did you identify this as a gap? Within organizations, a missing or incomplete picture of what the organization will look like in the next number of years is the most common limitation to inspiring a team or organization to achieve something great. Part of the reason most organizations lack a destination is the notion that defining your strategy is either too intimidating (feels like reading tea leaves to predict the future) or made out to be very complex (strategy experts are needed). Another reason for not having a strategic destination is it's easy to confuse an annual plan of what you want to accomplish as a strategy. But don't worry. If you have not defined a strategic destination, we'll guide you through a process to get there.

If you scored 4 to 5 on the above question resulting in a total score of 12 or more, you've indicated that your vision and culture are solid. Feel free to read through the vision exercise to pressure test both your vision and culture and move on to the next three elements.

Defining a Strategic Destination. In terms of defining a strategic destination, what may not be immediately apparent to most leaders, is you've likely already defined a strategy, albeit on a smaller scale. For this, we'll look at how we all build a micro-strategy: vacation planning. When you plan a vacation, there are three key elements:

1. What do you want to do?

2. Where do you want to go?

3. How do you want to get there?

Let's unpack these three parts of defining a strategic destination through the lens of vacation planning.

- *What do you want to do?* When daydreaming about a vacation, the first question to answer is what you want to do. Do you want to visit family, go to the beach, hike or ski in the mountains, explore a new city, or other options? The reason this is first is you don't decide to go to California if you really want to visit family in Florida or ski in the Alps.

- *Where do you want to go?* Once you know what you want to do, then you identify feasible options of where you want to go. Say you want to go to the beach and need to consider the available time and resources to get there. You may have a long weekend available (four days), and a budget that indicates a two-week trip to the Maldives is likely out. But a trip to a beach within a short flight or drive will work. Defining the destination requires a realistic assessment of the resources you have (more on that later).

- *How do you want to get there?* With the activities and location defined, now you define how you're going to get there. You may choose to take a flight, but do you want a direct flight or a flight with three connections to make the trip more affordable. Also you look at how you get to the airport (taxi or park at the airport). When you get to the destination, do you want to rent a car (and what type) or utilize local transportation? Planning how you get there also evaluates the approach that is best for your budget and preferences.

This example illustrates that if you have planned a vacation, you've built a strategy. The same three elements apply, but why is building a strategy in the business world perceived as so much harder? Let's take a look.

Defining What You Want to Do - SWOT Analysis. Many approaches are available to support strategic planning, but a common approach used to define strategic opportunities, the SWOT analysis looks for strengths, weaknesses, opportunities, and threats. We recommend each member of the leadership team independently define the strengths, weaknesses, opportunities, and threats for the overall organization. Here are definitions for the SWOT analysis.

- **Strengths.** What does the organization currently do well? Are there activities, services, processes, or products the organization is known to be experts in?

- **Weaknesses.** What does the organization not do well or which areas need to be improved?

- **Opportunities.** What external factors can the organization utilize to its advantage?

- **Threats.** What external factors could derail the progress or strengths of the organization today or in the future?

When the team members complete their individual SWOTs, we recommend a good amount of detail. For example if a team member writes "poor culture" as a threat, that will be difficult to define an action plan. Instead, if the same team member includes "poor work-life balance for team members" or "low morale due to long hours," these more specific items will be easier to address.

With the SWOT lists created, the team then comes together to compile into one master list. We added a template to help you document in the bonus resources (www.enlumagroup.com/book/), but many variants are available across the Internet. For the combined lists, the team will need to make some decisions and prioritize where to focus. Unless the team has unlimited resources, you will not be able to do everything.

With the initial discussion completed, the leadership team reviews the data together and defines the four to five key areas of focus. For example, the focus areas could include Financial Performance, People

Development, Data/Analytics, IT Systems, Process Improvements, etc. Each team member can create their initial list of four to five focus areas, review together and the organizational leader is the final approver. Then with the focus areas defined, what are the future destinations for each based on the analysis? Examples could include the following:

- Focus area: Culture

  o Future Destination: Make our organization a desired place for talent and growth and development.

- Focus area: IT Systems

  o Future Direction: Established best-in-class processes and then streamline to single IT systems to fully support our team members.

Going through this exercise, you'll notice there will be more energy and excitement around certain areas and less in others. In building your strategic destination, there should be positive energy around the areas where you'd like to focus and grow. You'll likely see key opportunities emerge which will lead to core strategies that the organization will want to pursue. Another recommendation for the leadership discussion is to balance realism with opportunity. Notice, we are not saying achieve consensus. What are the opportunities that may be a stretch and would set the organization up for long-term success? How do you identify those opportunities? You'll hear comments such as the following:

"It would be tough but amazing if we could accomplish (goal)."

"The broader team has been asking for (need) for years, and this would really enhance their performance."

"We'd all have to work closely together, but (new initiative) could be a game changer."

The tone of the discussion will be similar to what you see above. The destinations would not be easy but would be transformational. Then with a draft list of activities to complete for each of the focus areas, the team will then pressure test their initial destination.

Where do You Want to Go - Three-Year Visualization

We recommended that individually, each team member takes time to reflect and answer the following question:

It's three years from today, you're sitting at home reflecting on the past three years and are very proud of what the organization and leadership team has completed. What are one to two accomplishments that make you the most proud?

For these visualized future accomplishments, we recommend the organizational leader to really challenge the team for an exciting future and ask participants to be specific in what they see. The details include quantifiable targets for improvement, specific reactions or behaviors, and a detailed picture of how the organization has improved. With these specific insights, the team will then work together to consolidate and define the strategic destination of the organization. The analysis should include the following:

- What similarities and differences are observed between team members' visualizations, and why are they different? (goal of a detailed alignment)

- What surprises does the team see?

- What is missing that is surprising?

- What would excite and energize you?

- What would energize the broader organization?

Together as a team, work through defining each of the focus areas. This will then take the shape of your initial vision. The team will have one more question to consider.

How do You Want to Get There - Culture Visualization

Noting the vision, how should the broader organization operate (this leadership team included) to achieve the destination? In other words, what culture should be in place to ensure the future success?

Similar to the previous question about the three-year plans, the organizational leader asks the team to envision what they would consider a transformational culture and each team member should identify up to five specific elements of the culture that would enable the vision. The team should think about how they operate together and then how the broader organization should operate. This could include how team members operate from a day-to-day to year-to-year basis. With this question, team members can also leverage the SWOT analysis as an input to their comments.

Then the leadership team comes together and individually shares their insights. Similar to defining the vision, similar questions can enable the discussion such as the following:

- What similarities and differences are observed between team members' vision of the culture, and why are they different? (goal of a detailed alignment)

- What surprises does the team see? What would surprise the organization?

- What surprised the team that is missing?

- What would excite you about this culture?

- What are historical ways of operating ("the way we do things") that need to be addressed?

With these and similar questions, the overall characteristics of the desired culture start to take shape. The team works together on clarifying the culture and the organizational leader will ultimately approve it. Having the initial vision and the picture of the culture, more work is to come.

We recommend for the leadership to step back and take a look at the initial strategic destinations. To achieve these results:

- Which destinations will require a broader team (including team members from the organization to drive)?

- Which should be only led by the leadership team?

- In the vast majority of cases, a broader team can define the timelines and drive the improvements to improve momentum and take pressure off the leadership team.

- It's recommended that each member of the leadership team own or co-own one of the focus areas (ie, lead one of the broader teams).

This exercise is the first step to clarify what the future could look like and how the culture could enable the journey. Later after the three remaining elements we'll discuss how to get input from the broader organization and build momentum.

Now the team can work together to score the remaining three elements of Organizational Leadership.

Team First: Energize the Organization

If the organization is engaged and knows they can contribute to being part of the solution, this will be a catalyst to enhance the momentum forward. Everybody wins.

Statements to Score	Team Rating (1 to 5)
We regularly solve issues or challenges by engaging team members throughout the organization.	
The leadership team encourages a structure of healthy debate and considers different viewpoints.	
As an organization, we regularly balance the need to move fast with taking the time to understand issues/challenges.	
Total Score	

For the ratings 1 = Completely Disagree to 5 = Completely Agree

Accelerate: Illuminate the Path

With a future vision, do you want the broader organization to be an active participant on the journey? If you do, they need to know how to get there.

Statements to Score	Team Rating (1 to 5)
You are aligned on the "why" behind key goals and plans shared by the leadership team.	
You know how my goals tie to and support the future business success.	
The leadership team provides periodic updates to reinforce the desired future direction along with progress, and changes.	
Total Score	

For the ratings 1 = Completely Disagree to 5 = Completely Agree

Elevate: Be an Authentic Part of the Team

In thinking about being just one of the team and not more important than anyone else, you are more likely to better understand what is going on around the organization. This will help to see hurdles to the strategic vision and identify ways to help the broader organization.

Statements to Score	Team Rating (1 to 5)
The leadership team has demonstrated a strong grasp of the organization's strengths, challenges, and opportunities.	
The leadership team knows the resources and tools the organization needs to be successful.	
The leadership team regularly meets with team members to understand their roles and the daily challenges they encounter.	
Total Score	

For the ratings 1 = Completely Disagree to 5 = Completely Agree

The team has now completed both initial and final ratings for all four elements of the Organizational Leadership Layer. Specific to the organizational leader, we recommend you step back and align on the following questions:

1. Where do you see the biggest opportunities, and how does this differ with the feedback of the leadership team?

2. How could these opportunities impact the broader organization?

3. How would you like the leadership team to work together to continue to build momentum as a leadership team moving forward?

4. How are you going to engage and integrate the broader organization?

5. Compared to before starting this exercise, how has your outlook for the future changed? (Consider asking the leadership team the same question)

6. Where would you like the leadership team and the organization to be in three, six, or twelve months?

Additional Insights

Team First: We Win Together. For reasons that will become clear later, an organizational leader's best friend can be "We Win Together." When you define the destination, the team will then be part of defining the journey on how to make progress. Then good ideas will come in. However, if this is a big change from the past, the organization will understandably be very skeptical that leadership (including you) will listen, let alone act on their feedback. As a result, the tactical piece here is key. For example, if you want to improve the culture and ensure "We Win Together," can you get feedback from some focus groups in the organization to understand how you currently address issues/challenges? The goal is to understand whether good ideas are surfacing and if they are not, what is preventing them from being shared. Ideas and sometimes transformational ideas are out there. You need to ensure good ideas are surfacing.

Accelerate: Illuminate the Path. With the communication plan for the future, the broader organization will likely want to know the following:

- What does this mean for their day-to-day work? Most people think short term because this is how we live. The team will want to know how this will disrupt their lives, including number of hours, changes in pay, or other changes.

- How will this make their lives better? Will there be new growth opportunities for team members or a chance for more pay? Will this increase the likelihood of long-term survival of the team and if relevant, the viability of the organization?

- Will there be any negative consequences (cost savings or layoffs)? This may not be everyone, but odds are, there will be at least a few people who are wondering if the future state strategy is all lip service benefiting leadership more than the broader organization.

- Is the leadership team really serious? There may have been past "strategies" that were put in place, and they may have been successful (that's a plus), or they may have been unfulfilled and deprioritized by other issues. The organization will not know if the leadership is serious until actions are implemented starting generating momentum.

Elevate: Be an Authentic Part of the Team. Earlier in the book we shared the Teddy Roosevelt quote, "Nobody will care what you know, until they know that you care." Especially if you are new to being an organizational leader or had challenges in the past, the team at best, doesn't know if you care. One tool in your toolbox to remedy this, sit with the team members while they are doing the work to observe. You don't need to spend a lot of time; it could be thirty minutes a week. Here are the key parts:

- Be present. Stay off your phone, don't check emails, and don't have the team member come to you. Go to them where they work.

- Listen and ask questions from a place of curiosity. You're trying to better understand the team members and what issues or concerns they have with their work. They will likely ask you questions.

If you're able to find thirty minutes a week, you'll find these insights are invaluable. You'll be more aware of what is going on with the organization and the team will note that "the boss" was sitting with the team. Now will the team be completely honest and open? Probably not to start. With time, the team members will likely start to open up. If you as the leader don't know about challenges and problems, then how can you help to fix them?

Step 2: Share the initial strategic destination and culture expectations with the organization.

Enluma Experience: Chris

In the call center role, I along with the leadership team I had the opportunity to lead utilized a SWOT analysis to better understand opportunities and help us to prioritize and build our strategy. It was a good first effort, but we didn't consider the vision completed. Next each manager shared the vision with their teams and asked for input. What concerns did they have? Did they like where we were going? How did this really help? The organization pressure tested the strategy. Did we get some critical constructive feedback about timelines and feasibility? Absolutely, and we updated our plan to make it more robust.

The story helps illustrate that getting feedback before the vision is completed can be powerful. This is also key for building momentum and trust. Genuinely pressure-test the vision with the organization. This also helps to identify where teams are needed to progress elements of the vision and culture.

At this point, you may think you can just go ahead and share the vision with the organization. Ahead of the collective reveal, you need to establish your infrastructure to collect ideas (where the organization wins together) and define how ideas will be reviewed, prioritized, and implemented. Here's the reason why: you're working on the destination for the organization and will have some initial plans on how the organization will get there. Sample destinations for a focus area could include the following:

(a) Focus Area: Sales Performance

Destination: Be the sales leader (for your product) in Germany by unlocking the full potential of the sales organization.

(b) Focus Area: Culture

Destination: Elevate decision making and proactive thinking to significantly reduce fire-fighting by XX percent.

(c) Focus Area: Customer Impact

Destination: Be the most subscribed YouTube channel for "at-home" cooking.

The clear destination includes a detailed description. To realize the future, you'll need ideas from the broader organization. There are a variety of ways to collect ideas and the approach can be adjusted based on the existing culture.

Enluma Experience: Chris

In the call center, we leveraged a Think Tank event that we called "Innovation Day," where once a month any team member could present ideas to a diverse panel (not just leadership), and they would get approval on the spot to move forward. We also had a continuous improvement team, encouraged sharing of information in 1:1s or team meetings, and provided updates in all employee meetings. The broader team shared feedback that they appreciated being part of the process, even if a leadership team had the final say.

With options for collections of ideas identified, then you determine how you prioritize and rate the ideas. It could tie to feasibility, impact, and cost. You'll also need to plan who will prioritize (hint: it doesn't need to rest solely on the leadership team). With all of this, a simpler process for collecting and evaluating ideas is key so it doesn't risk becoming cumbersome.

With the plan in place to collect ideas, now you're ready to share the initial plan. Although the team has likely seen it before, the goal is to collectively present the plan and reinforce the leadership team will be looking for ideas to progress the vision forward. It's also a good time to share which of the leadership team will be owning or co-owning a focus area and where teams will be in place to drive progress.

Third step: Plan for keeping the progress alive and evolving while integrating into your identity as an organization.

Inspiring an organization to learn more, dream more, do more and become more is a marathon and not a sprint. There will be some initial gains up front, especially with including the organization and making progress. The challenge now becomes how to make this a part of the organization's identity, to make it sustainable. You run the risk of another issue or different priority coming along and derailing the focus on continuous improvement. To prevent this from happening, here are some considerations:

- **Measuring and communicating progress.** This vision represents the future of the organization. It's critical to determine key milestones and objectives that are coming up and how you want to communicate and track and ensure they happen

- **Periodic (ideally quarterly) review.** With the leadership team (and ideally the extended leadership team) review the strategic destination, and have honest discussions about progress (good or bad) and whether course corrections are needed.

  o The other element of this destination is the rolling 3-year plan. On a periodic basis, review (1) what was completed,

(2) what was missed, (3) what needs to be adjusted, and (4) what will be further improved for the third year.

○ Similarly, an annual review of the plan can be integrated into the annual goal planning process, financial processes, and team performance management.

○ This approach then becomes part of the organization's DNA.

- **Annual rebrand and update.** People will typically stay interested in a program or branded activity for about a year. On an annual basis, consider changing the look and feel of the program to realize the strategy/vision. This can also include dividing each year or defining key phases. This will then break up the journey into portions.

- **Celebrations and recognition.** With the majority of the organization on board, plan celebrations when progress is achieved, and provide recognition for teams or team members that are making significant contributions. This positive reinforcement can be really appreciated and add fun.

- **Team specificity.** What motivates and energizes an organization can vary. Some will want a large group gathering, and others may want more time with their family. The leadership team should adjust their approach to the organization as opposed to trying to adjust the organization.

Stepping Back

Looking at the planning for the journeys, you may have noticed a trend. The amount of effort needed to be inspirational for a foundational leader is less than a people leader, and these are both less than for an organizational leader. All of these journeys are truly built on Foundational Leadership to start. Noting this trend of the large effort needed for an organizational leader to be inspirational illustrates why so few organizational leaders take the action. In fact, in 2023 McKinsey analyzed the state of c-suite leadership in nearly 400 different organizations[41]. What percent of senior leaders do you think were inspirational and fit for purpose as defined by their own company feedback? Only 25 percent. That's a huge opportunity to elevate organizational leadership.

We have had the opportunity to put these principles into action. Intentionality and sustained focus are absolutely required. Ironically though, once you put practices in place, there is a huge weight lifted off your shoulders. The organization is engaged, direct reports are growing, and you're working collaboratively with peers. Yes, there are ups and downs, good days and bad days. But collectively, it's amazing.

So, we are challenging you. If you're in, take the next 30 days and pressure test the approach with the organization leadership team If the team doesn't buy into the approach, then minimal time is lost. Our guess is the team will see the benefit and want to move forward, so much so that you'll want to progress the journey.

We challenge you. Are you ready to take on the challenge?

Conclusion

We started this book with five nagging questions that we wanted to answer. Four out of the five we covered extensively:

- When people say "leader," what do they mean?

We aligned on the definition from John Quincy Adams, "If your actions inspire others to dream more, learn more, do more, and become more, then you're a leader". This establishes THE concise definition for what is an inspirational leader.

- **Why don't we have a model enabling the development of inspirational leaders?**

- **What are the key elements of inspirational leadership?**

- **How can we more intentionally develop leaders who energize and inspire?**

In response to these three questions, we introduced and covered the Enluma Leadership Model illustrating a practical method to develop more inspirational leaders. We also identified the four elements of an inspirational leader: Team First, Accelerate, Elevate, and Realize. With the leadership layers, we presented the differences in leading yourself and others (Foundational Leadership), direct teams (People Leadership), and multiple levels of people (Organizational Leadership). The power of questions unlocks the model, so every leader can provide answers to be part of the solution and leverage the same questions to develop and challenge others. And the glue that holds it all together: trust and fun.

That leaves us with one remaining unanswered question:

- **Why don't we expect that every group is successful, fulfilling, and enjoyable?**

This is a question we need to ask ourselves and consider the possibilities. Going through the book, we talk about the different layers separately, but what happens if you look at inspirational leadership collectively across the layers. You see the possibilities and the impact we can all have.

If I worked for an organization that utilized the Enluma Leadership Model, then I would expect my peers to be looking out for me and willingly share information. I would expect my direct manager is looking to develop me as I work toward being my best. Additionally, in the organization, I would know where we are going (supporting the powerful destination) and the expected culture on how to be successful. Knowing where we are going and how we are working together, I can then see opportunities that will both help me grow and progress in line with the direction of the organization. We all know there are no perfect jobs, but in this environment, I would very likely be energized and motivated to make an impact. I would know that I am part of something bigger than myself.

If I had the opportunity to lead a direct team in the same Enluma-powered organization, I would see everything from an individual perspective noted above, and I'd see more engaged direct team members. Direct team members who know I am helping and challenging them to be their best. A team that knows the expectation is for them to work together and help each other. Since we know where the organization is going, our staff meetings are more aligned to the vision as we make progress. Because I work to see myself as part of the team (not the most important person), direct team members will challenge me and each other to make sure we're moving forward. As we make progress, we celebrate together and build increased momentum.

Then if I had an opportunity to lead an organization utilizing the Enluma model, we would have established a clear direction for the future and defined expectations for our culture where we empower team members to work together and come up with solutions. I should spend less time on firefighting and have more time focused on the culture and strategy to better anticipate and prepare us for the future. Yes there will be challenges where I will need to be aware and help the team, but I don't need to spend the majority of my time micro-managing the day-to-day. This approach will also help me as a people leader because it will free up time to develop the direct team, so I can practice what we are preaching to the broader organization. I can also spend more time with my peers to make sure we act on opportunities to better partner together.

As you likely also gathered from reading this book, implementing the Enluma Leadership Model in organizations will have transformational effects. Throughout our careers, we have been able to achieve astonishing results in different organizations, countries, and programs in Fortune 100 companies. Based on our experience, we also know that not everyone will be a good fit with the Enluma model. Individuals who are addicted to fire-fighting or enjoy creating drama, will not be a good fit. Leaders of organizations who want to see themselves as the most important part of the team or who only know and trust old-school, command-and-control approaches intended to squeeze productivity out of team members are unlikely to truly adopt the Enluma Leadership Model. Unfortunately, these team members and leaders will be missing out on a significant opportunity.

With the Enluma Leadership Model, we expect groups to be energized and motivated. We expect people to be more driven and look to see how they could contribute to help the team realize a meaningful future, how they could grow to build their skill sets to make a broader impact, and how they could work to be their best and inspire others to do the same. We expect online company reviews to describe whether the company and the leaders are inspirational. Based on our experience, we would also expect to see a strong correlation of company success and employee satisfaction with implementation of the Enluma Leadership Model. In short, we believe utilization of inspirational leadership through the Enluma Leadership Model can provide a competitive advantage for any organization in achieving results, developing and retaining talent, growing your organization, and achieving employee satisfaction.

This is the future we see. This is the future we are working to unlock. This is the future every organization and employee deserves. **Inspirational leadership is THE KEY to make the improbable possible.**

Bibliography

Introduction

No references

Part 1: The Current State of Leadership

Chapter 1 – A Leader's Impact

1. Colin Powell with Joseph E Persico, My American Journey, Ballantine Books, NY, 1ˢᵗ revised ed, 2003.

2. https://www.youtube.com/watch?v=PbfBUrh4QWM&t=12s

3. Latest Corporate Crisis: Only 11% of Surveyed Companies Have a Strong Leadership Bench, Fortune Magazine, May 19, 2021. Edward Segal.

4. Horrible Bosses: Are American Workers Quitting Their Jobs or Quitting Their Managers, Goodhire Research Article, Sara Korolevich, 11 January 2022. (https://www.goodhire.com/resources/articles/horrible-bosses-survey/)

5. Proof That Positive Work Cultures Are More Productive, Emma Seppala and Kim Cameron, Harvard Business Review, 01 December 2015, Published on HBR.org, Reprint H02IMC.

6. What is the True Cost of Work-Related Stress, The American Institute of Stress. April 20, 2022. https://www.stress.org/news/what-is-the-true-cost-of-work-related-stress/#:~:text=One%20notable%20cost%2Dof%2Dillness,absenteeism%2C%20turnover%2C%20diminished%20productivity%2C

7. Treating Employees Well Led to Higher Stock Prices During the Pandemic, Great Places to Work, Marcus Erb, 05 Aug 2021 (https://www.greatplacetowork.com/resources/blog/treating-employees-well-led-to-higher-stock-prices-during-the-pandemic)

8. https://www.gettysburg.edu/news/stories?id=79db7b34-630c-4f49-ad32-4ab9ea48e72b#:~:text=The%20average%20person%20will%20spend%2090%2C000%20hours%20at%20work%20over%20a%20lifetime.

9. What Millennials Want from a New Job, Harvard Business Review, Brandon Rigoni and May Adkins, Harvard Business Review, 11 May 2016.

10. LiveCareer's Different Generations in the Workplace 2024 Study. https://www.livecareer.com/resources/careers/planning/generation-diversity-in-the-workplace

Chapter 2 - What Is a Leader?

11. Oxford Online Dictionary: (https://languages.oup.com/google-dictionary-en/)

12. The 21 Irrefutable Laws of Leadership, John C Maxwell, Hachette Book Group, 10th Anniversary Edition, 2021.

Part 2: The Enluma Leadership Model

Chapter 3 – Introduction to the Enluma Leadership Model

13. Steve Hatfield, Sue Cantrell, and Corrie Commisso, Outcomes over outputs, Why productivity is no longer the metric that matters most. Deloitte Insights Magazine, Issue 32, 19 July 2023.

14. Marilee Adams, Change Your Questions Change Your Life, Barrett-Koehler Publishers, 2015.

15. Michael Bungay Stanier, The Coaching Habit, Page Two Books, 2016

Chapter 4 – Inspirational Leadership Elements

16. James Kouzes and Barry Posner, The Leadership Challenge, 2023, Jossey-Bass, 7th Edition.

17. Jon Katzenbach and Douglas Smith, The Wisdom of Teams,

18. Charles Duhigg, What Google Learned From Its Quest to Build the Perfect Team, the New York Times Magazine, 25 February 2016.

19. Anita Williams Woolley, et al, Evidence for a Collective Intelligence Factor in Performance of Human Groups, Science, Vol 330, 29 Oct 2010, p. 686 – 688.

20. Ana Mayo and Anita Williams Woolley, Teamwork in Healthcare: Maximizing Collective Intelligence via Inclusive Collaboration and Open Communication. 2016. The AMA Journal of Ethic, Vol 18, No 9, 933-940.

Chapter 5 – Leadership Layers and the Combined Enluma Leadership Model

21. How to Lead Your Fellow Rainmakers, Harvard Business Review, Laura Empson, March-April 2019.

22. Havana Arora, Importance of Emotional Intelligence in the Workplace, International Journal of Engineering and Applied Sciences, vol 4, Iss 4, April 2017. Pages 43 to 45.

23. On Emotional Intelligence, HBRs 10 Must Reads, Harvard Business Review Press, 2015.

24. Daryl Bem, Self-Perception: An alternative interpretation of cognitive dissonance phenomena. Psychology Review, 1967, Vol 74, No 3, 183-200.

25. Kristin D Neff, Kristin L Kirkpatrick, and Stephanie S Rude, Self-Compassion and Adaptive Psychological Functioning. Journal of Research in Personality, Vol. 41, 2007, p. 139-154.

26. Timothy Clark, The 4 Stages of Psychological Safety, National Geographic Books, 2020.

27. Christine Porath and Christine Pearson, The Price of Incivility, Harvard Business Review, Jan-Feb 2013.

28. Stephen Covey, Seven Habits of Highly Effective People, Free Press, 1989.

Chapter 6 - Leadership Glue

29. Lionel P Robert, Alan R Dennis, and Tu-Ting Caisy Hung (2009), Individual Swift Trust and Knowledge-Based Trust in Face-to-Face Virtual Team Members, Journal of Management Information, vol 26, No 2, 241-279.

30. Judith, A Holton, 2001, Building Trust and Collaboration in a Virtual Team, Terra Performance Management, Vol, 7, No ¾, p 36-47.

31. What is a Gemba Walk and Why is it Important? Six Sigma Daily, 17 January 2018. https://www.sixsigmadaily.com/what-is-a-gemba-walk/

32. Ted Lasso, Episode 9, Season 1, Ted Lasso, Apple TV, 2020.

33. Ted Lasso, Episode 12, Season 2, Ted Lasso, Apple TV, 2021.

34. Roula Amire and Great Place to Work, Fun Drives high levels of well-being at the Best Workplaces for Millennials, Fortune Magazine, (https://fortune.com/2023/07/18/fun-well-being-best-workplaces-millennials/)

35. Bob Nelson and Mario Tamayo, Work Made Fun Gets Done, National Geographic Books, May 2021.

36. CPP, Inc (Meyers-Briggs), Workplace Conflict and How Business Can Harness it to Thrive, July 2008. (https://shop.themyersbriggs.com/pdfs/cpp_global_human_capital_report_workplace_conflict.pdf)

Part 3 - The Enluma Leadership Model in Practice

Chapter 7 – Foundational Leadership

No references

Chapter 8 – People Leadership

No references

Chapter 9 – Organizational Leadership

No references

Part 4: Your Journey

Chapter 10 – The Destination and the Plan

37. Stacey McLachlan (2021) The Science of habit: What does it take to stick with something long term? You just have to rewire your brain. Healthline, (medically reviewed by. Debra Rose Wilson) (https://www.healthline.com/health/the-science-of-habit#1)

38. Sabina Nawaz, 2020, To Achieve Big Goals, Start with Small Habits, Harvard Business Review, 20 January 2020.

39. Sabina Nawaz, 2022, To Build New Habits, Get Comfortable Failing, Harvard Business Review, 21 January 2022.

Chapter 11 - Enluma Leadership Model for Foundational Leadership

No references

Chapter 12 - Enluma Leadership Model for People Leadership

No references

Chapter 13 - Enluma Leadership Model for People Leadership

40. McKinsey State of Organizations 2023, Leadership that is Self-Aware and Inspiring, p. 37 to 41. (https://www.mckinsey.com/capabilities/people-and-organizational-performance/our-insights/the-state-of-organizations-2023)

Appendix A

Background Data from Study on Productive and Positive Workgroups

Of the 421 people we surveyed, our target was to get a variety of experiences, especially related to the number of direct supervisors. Here are the key demographics of the participants:

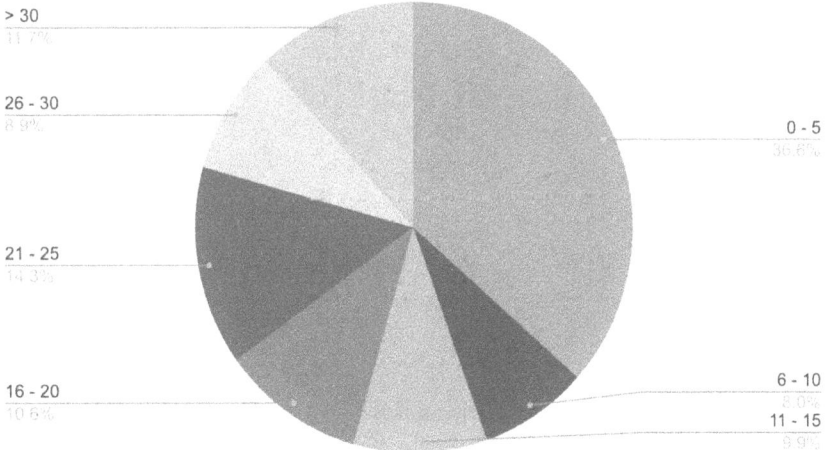

Years of Experience

Our survey participants leaned more toward the 0–5 years of experience range; however, we had a good distribution of the number of direct supervisors per respondent.

Number of Direct Supervisors

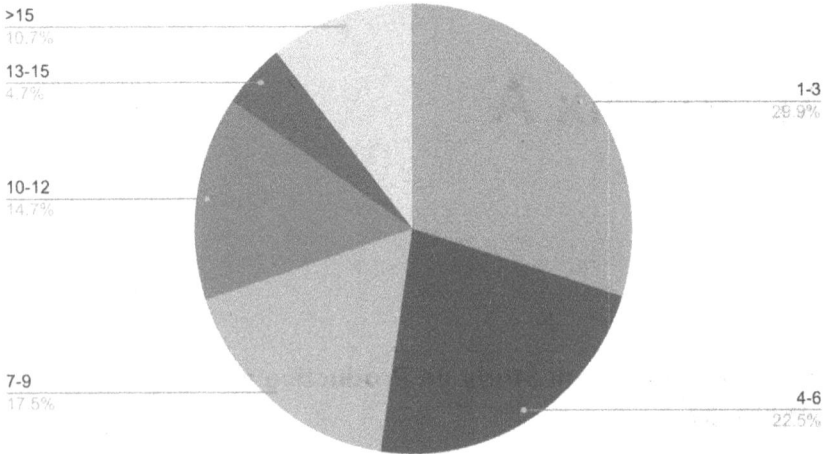

>15
10.7%

13-15
4.7%

10-12
14.7%

7-9
17.5%

1-3
29.9%

4-6
22.5%

We also looked at the number of job titles or roles per respondent.

Number of job titles/roles per respondent

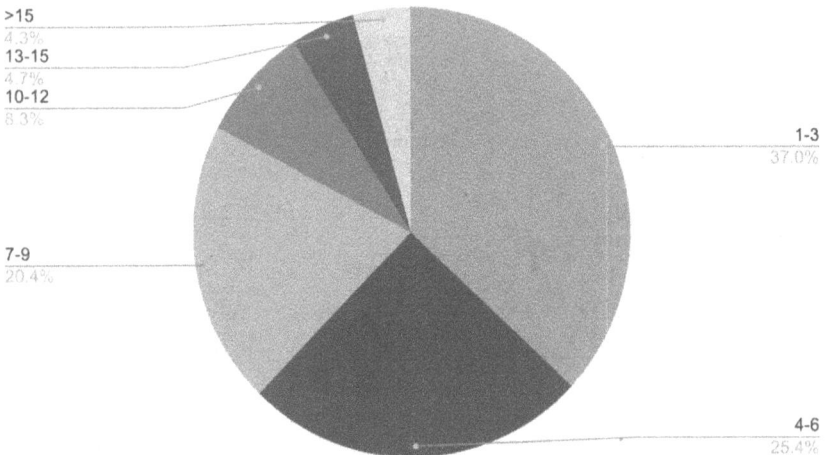

>15
4.3%
13-15
4.7%
10-12
8.3%

7-9
20.4%

1-3
37.0%

4-6
25.4%

Here we also saw a good distribution while we were a little skewed to the lower end of the range, suggesting people likely have more direct supervisors than roles.

In terms of education background, we also saw a variety of different backgrounds:

Education Background (highest degree achieved) of Participants

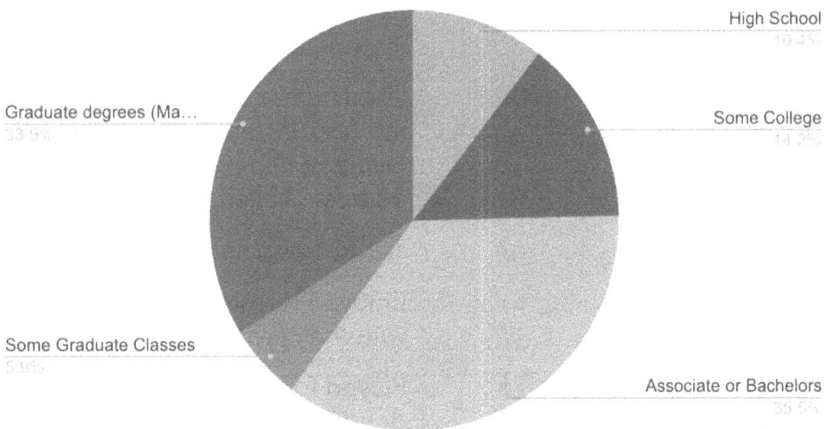

With this diversity of backgrounds, we then asked how many of the 422 respondents said they had experienced a productive and enjoyable workgroup, 374 (88.6 percent) indicated yes for one or more of these groups. This was much higher than we had anticipated. Elements Observed with Study Evaluating Positive and Productive Workgroups

Inspirational Element	# of Responses	Criteria for Response
Realize a meaningful goal	138	Combination of two factors had to be present: (1) having a clear or well understood goal and (2) hard working, making progress or forward momentum

Inspirational Element	# of Responses	Criteria for Response
Unify - team first	105	Team focused, didn't want to let others down, part of the team
Elevate through partnership	104	Helping each other, looking out for each other, noting each others' needs
Accelerate with data	99	Strong communication, very clear expectations, constantly sharing information
Positive attitude and used humor	80	Used humor or a positive attitude, including how to leverage humor / attitude to address challenges
Trust	62	Trust or respect noted
Learning and asking questions	61	Enjoyed learning and growing with the challenge
Understanding and utilizing each other strengths	26	Played to each other's strengths or utilized the talents of others
Humility	11	Mentioned humility or humbleness
Agility or rlexibility	10	Noted agility, flexibility or something similar
Rewards or recognition	4	Received awards, praise, or recognition for the work
Executive support	4	Strong support from leaders above my immediate supervisor

The criteria on the right was the defined search criteria utilized to quantify the responses. If a response was not clear such as "we worked hard" or "everyone was competent," then to be conservative the response was not included in the responses.

About the Author

Christopher L. Sprague, PhD, CEO of the Enluma Leadership Group and co-developer of the Enluma Leadership Model, is dedicated to transforming the future of work focused primarily on achieving incredible results in a sustainable and healthy way enabling long-term success. Drawing on his extensive experience across diverse industries and multiple Fortune 100 companies, Christopher aims to drive positive, lasting change. His mission is to cultivate leadership excellence at all organizational levels, fostering a global culture of inspirational leadership. He holds a bachelor's degree from the University of Delaware and a PhD from the University of Wisconsin-Madison.

Contributing Author

Jan Leeuwinga, MBA, co-developer of the Enluma Leadership Model, has a deep passion for strategy development, organizational growth, and forging genuine connections with team performance and advancement. Drawing from his extensive 25-year career across diverse industries, cultures, and challenging roles, he aims to make the improbable possible through inspirational leadership, driving fundamental transformation in organizations, teams, and individuals. Jan studied at the Northern Academy of Logistics in the Netherlands and earned his MBA from the Lake Forest Graduate School of Management.

www.ingramcontent.com/pod-product-compliance
Lightning Source LLC
Chambersburg PA
CBHW011159220326
41597CB00026BA/4674